What To Do When You're
Scared To Death

Pat Palau
and PeggySue Wells

MONARCH
BOOKS
Oxford, UK & Grand Rapids, Michigan, USA

First published in the UK in 2008 by Monarch Books
(a publishing imprint of Lion Hudson plc),
Wilkinson House, Jordan Hill Road, Oxford OX2 8DR.
Tel: +44 (0)1865 302750 Fax: +44 (0)1865 302757
Email: monarch@lionhudson.com
www.lionhudson.com

ISBN: 978-1-85424-887-9 (UK)
ISBN: 978-0-8254-6293-1 (USA)

Distributed by:
UK: Marston Book Services Ltd, PO Box 269, Abingdon, Oxon OX14 4YN;
USA: Kregel Publications, PO Box 2607, Grand Rapids, Michigan 49501

British Library Cataloguing Data
A catalogue record for this book is available from the British Library.

Printed and bound in England by CPI Cox & Wyman

Dedication

I don't know why I choose to write on a subject that I have not yet conquered. I suppose many subjects of vital usefulness would never be dealt with if we waited until we had it all together, and figured out.

In our forty-seven years of marriage, I learned early to "lean on the everlasting arms" as I watched Luis set a wonderful example. Looking into his eyes, I have been strengthened in realizing that he believes that God will undertake for all our fears, and provide for all our needs.

Because he believes, I am strengthened to trust along with him. All over the world, he has believed that millions need to be delivered from the fear of death, "all their lifetime subject to bondage," and I have been blessed to tag along.

The journey's not over. We move along a path from fear to faith.

PAT

To my courageous children, AmyRose, Leilani, Holly, Josiah, Estee, Hannah, and Lilyanna. And to those who have exemplified courage to me, Dr Joe and Shirley Martin, Dennis and Rose Hensley, Char and Steve Binkley, and, of course, Chip and Patti MacGregor.

PEGGYSUE

Contents

Acknowledgments

I would just thank PeggySue for putting the wind beneath my wings. No way would, or could, I have ever gotten anything like this done without you. What you know, and can accomplish is just totally out of my skill set. It is a two-girl job.

PAT

One of the best perks of publishing a book is having the opportunity to acknowledge some amazing and courageous people. Topping that list is the single-focused Luis and his spunky wife, Pat Palau, their sons and daughters-in-law, grandbabies, and many friends and supporters who care deeply about serving up generous portions of the Good News to everyone worldwide. Luis and Pat are a couple who heard the Good Shepherd's voice early, responded eagerly, and have faithfully followed his calling.

Many thanks for the efforts of our agent, Chip MacGregor, who heard my persistent calls and agreed to connect this project with a publisher who shared the same passion.

Our appreciation reaches across the pond to Lion Hudson, who are passionate about sharing Jesus Christ with the world through the vehicle of the printed word. Their partnership gives wings to this book, as they send it to the nations.

PEGGYSUE

FOREWORD

It was 1981. My wife, Pat, and I were in Glasgow, Scotland, for the final days of a massive, six-week, nation-wide evangelistic campaign. Having spent the first five weeks at home with our young boys, Pat joined me for the final gatherings. But she wasn't her normal, cheerful self. After two days I finally mustered the courage to ask what was wrong. I wasn't ready for her response.

"There is a lump," she said. "I fear the worst."

I was speechless. My wife? Cancer? Could it really be possible? I tried not to jump to conclusions, but my mind swirled. And yet, surprisingly, Pat seemed peaceful in the midst of this potentially fatal discovery.

Arriving home in Portland, Oregon, we immediately went to see the doctor. He took a biopsy and told us to return on Thursday for the results. In the meantime, we were on our knees. We prayed and hoped that it wasn't malignant.

However, on Thursday, the look on the doctor's face told us the news wasn't good. Tests showed a serious, malignant tumor, and he recommended immediate surgery.

We sat there, our world crashing around us.

We left the doctor's office and headed to the car.

Finally, my beautiful wife broke the silence: "Well, this is it. This is the end."

"No," I replied, "this is not the end. We still have the boys to bring up. We still have many dreams that the Lord has laid on our hearts. I think you will be healed and we will serve the Lord together for many years to come."

Deep down, I'm not sure if I really believed that at the time, but in my heart I was building up my own faith while hoping it to be true.

When we got home, the boys were still at school. Pat and I decided to take some time alone to process the day's events. I went to the basement of our home and without letting Pat see, I broke down. In the midst of tears and prayers, I heard music. It was coming from the piano in the living-room.

Pat was playing the old hymns she had learned in church as a little girl: "Under His Wings I'm Safely Abiding"; "The Church's One Foundation is Jesus Christ Her Lord".

I was stunned. She had just found out she had a cancerous tumor, and she was singing to Jesus Christ. Yet, isn't this exactly what we've always believed – that our time is in his hands, that God makes no mistakes, that his permissive will is often mysterious, and yet nevertheless our lives are in the hands of a merciful, sovereign God who knows our going in and our coming out? He understands his purposes for the long range. How amazing that this woman, my wife, received horrendous news and her first instinct was to praise her Savior and Lord.

We called the elders of the church. They came to the hospital on Sunday, prayed over her and anointed her with oil as Scripture instructs. We asked forgiveness for any sins there might be. Then we committed her to the Lord.

By God's grace, she went into surgery free of fear.

Hours later, Pat emerged from surgery a bit disoriented. When she finally came to, she shared, "I felt such peace. I felt like God had embraced me and held me close to himself, just like my dad used to do when I was a little girl."

I remembered the words of Psalm 91:

He who dwells in the shelter of the Most High, who abides in the shadow of the Almighty, will say to the Lord, "My refuge and my fortress; my God, in whom I trust." For he will deliver you from the snare of the fowler and from the deadly pestilence; he will cover you with his pinions, and under his wings you will find refuge; his faithfulness is a shield and buckler. You will not fear the terror of the night, nor the arrow that flies by day, nor the pestilence that stalks in darkness, nor the destruction that wastes at noonday.

Following recovery, Pat came home. Then came the difficult, trying period of chemotherapy. She shivered from the cold – nothing could make her feel warm. It wasn't easy, but she was strong. And her reliance on the Lord grew daily.

One day, a godly friend brought a carving with the words "God is able" lifted from 2 Corinthians 9:8. My wife took it to be a word from the Lord that he was not only able to heal her, but he would!

During the days of recuperation, we received literally hundreds of letters and cards, with one verse repeated over and over: "'For I know the plans I have for you,' declares the Lord, 'plans to prosper you and not to harm you, plans to give you hope and a future'" (Jeremiah 29:11).

The Lord proved true. It's been more than a quarter century since that trying incident. And we praise God every day.

What impacted me most was my wife's reaction throughout the whole ordeal. It was clear that God's peace surrounded her, filling her mind and heart.

Our lives are not always easy. My wife is a testament to that. Not only has she suffered through cancer, she has spent many lonely days on the mission field. Over the years I have been gone for long stretches, doing the ministry of evangelism. Humanly speaking, as she stayed home with our children in foreign lands (one of them a particularly violent society), she did not have the kind of protection that a husband would like to provide for his wife. Yet her trust in the Lord, her confidence in his protection, gave her a way to handle the normal, natural fears that all of us experience.

As you read her thoughts and biblical understanding, her knowledge of God and the reality of danger, illness, and other frightening situations, you will be blessed. Her insight and wisdom encourage you to think God's thoughts and to overcome your own fears – to the glory of the Lord.

In this book you will read more about her experience, how she handled it by faith in the Lord, trust in the Word of God, reliance on the character of God, and dependence on the promises of God.

Read on and then pass along this book as a gift. Through this book, your friends and relatives may find "the peace of God that transcends all understanding" (Philippians 4:7).

LUIS PALAU

So do not fear, for I am with you;
Do not be dismayed, for I am your God.
I will strengthen you and help you;
I will uphold you with my righteous right hand.

ISAIAH 41:10

INTRODUCTION

Child of my love, fear not the unknown morrow,
Dread not the new demand life makes on thee;
Thy lack of knowledge holds no cause for sorrow,
Since what thou knowest not is known to Me.

Thou canst not see today the hidden meaning
Of My command, but thou the light shalt gain.
Walk on in faith, upon My promise leaning,
And as thou goest, all shall be made plain.

Wherefore go gladly to the task assigned thee,
Having My promise, needing nothing more
Than just to know where e'er the future finds thee,
In all thy journeying I go before.

"As Thou Goest",
FROM THE NOTEBOOK OF ARTHUR E. RITCHIE

Not long ago, I collaborated with my husband in writing a booklet titled *How to Lead Your Child To Christ*. After it was published, I read it. In addition to excellent illustrations, it was a fine explanation about the salvation process, and the minds of little children. It talked all around the subject, but you couldn't say it clearly told you how to lead your child to Christ. Close, but no cigar.

Therefore, at the beginning of this book, so I can sleep nights, here are the most helpful answers to *What to Do When You're Scared to Death*. There are several key, God-given helps you will say you already knew. All of us know answers, but appropriating them is another story. Too often we are blind to the obvious and go off beating the bushes for something new, easy, and trendy when God has given us resources to deal with fear in his Word.

1. The *first* place to look for comfort, peace, and perspective is the instruction manual that came with the product (us!) – the Bible. According to some young women I met in a Bible study in India, there are 365 variations on the theme of fear in Scripture. God knows fear is very daily. Then and now. There and here.

2. Talk to God about the specific fear you face. Put it out in front of you and him where the two of you can view it clearly. God is not surprised or shocked. He already knows.

3. Find practical, tangible ways to make progress. Fear incapacitates; it strangles the life out of us. This book will provide steps to get you moving again – *despite* your fear and *through* your fear.

4. Recognize that to live in fear of man or beast is to fail to trust God. Failing to trust God leads to making excuses and blaming others. Remember

how Adam blamed Eve and Eve blamed
serpent. The bottom line was that they di
God's Word – what God had said (Genesis

5. Be patient. Fear, acknowledgment, and t⸺ing
tangible steps forward become a lifestyle of
growth and change.

6. Be prepared. Practice ahead of time. It's
not a case of *if* but *when*. God gives seasons
of peace when we tend to float along with the
naïve assumption that this state of affairs is our
God-given permanent right. Ephesians 6:13
talks about the evil day that inevitably comes:
"Therefore put on the full armor of God, so that
when the day of evil comes, you may be able
to stand your ground, and after you have done
everything, to stand."

"Remember your Creator in the days of your youth,
before the days of trouble come," Ecclesiastes 12:1 instructs.
Be armed daily with the full armor of God (Ephesians
6:10–18). Study the Scriptures and diligently hide
God's Word in your heart (Psalm 119:11).

In my comfortable pew, worshipping in the same
church most of my life gives me a long view. I see
the hand of God at work, changing me, weakening
the hold that my serious and silly fears have on me. I
cannot urge you onto a path I have never taken. If you
have the impression that I write because I understand
and have conquered all varieties of fear, I have misled
you. I am a fellow traveler, a follower of the Lord Jesus

...rist, always a learner. My desire is simply that you would keep your eyes on the Savior, and like Simon Peter, step out of the boat, and walk on water.

Peter succeeded, as long as he kept his eyes on Jesus, literally and figuratively. As we all know, when Peter took a look around to evaluate his situation, he began to sink. Jesus reached out and grabbed his hand, stabilizing Peter and getting him back into the boat. No rebuke. Jesus knows our frame and remembers we are but dust (Psalm 103). Peter's failure was not fatal. It was a step of growth.

You will quickly realize that I am not a professional counselor, nor a mental health specialist, only a fellow traveler on a journey away from the domination and control of fear. I'm not sure how to draw the line regarding normal fear and abnormal. The Bible uses the phrase "and such as is common to man" (1 Corinthians 10:13). When our fears move beyond our control for any length of time, it may be time to involve a mature follower of Christ to help us evaluate our situation.

In my young mothering days, I was expecting a fourth child, entering a new mission location, while all our worldly goods were held up somewhere on a ship for almost a year. I struggled to let go of fear and frustration. The stress was not unreasonable but my inability to let even resolved issues go was. I rehashed with my husband my inability to manage. He reminded me of several aspects of this situation that had already been resolved.

This was a warning to me; it's one thing to worry

and fret about reality, and quite another to just keep the mental machinery going, around real and exaggerated concerns. Rather like the busy hamster on his little wheel. He is going nowhere but he seems to enjoy the experience.

The answer for me was a change of scenery, orchestrated by a sensitive husband. I returned from a visit to my parents in the United States ready to tackle a new culture with renewed confidence in the God who had called us.

What I am saying is that there may be times when the listening and discerning ear of a professional person is warranted. But, behind it all, God is still our ultimate Refuge and Strength.

Sin is man's failure to trust in God. Sin is an act or state of unbelief. Sin is our assertion of autonomy. A healthy relationship with God is based on trusting him. Out of that trust, we obey him. God has all the time in the world and he doesn't give up on his greatest project – you!

Chapter 1

Garden Variety Fears

From ghoulies and ghosts
And long-legged beasties
And things that go bump in the night
Good Lord, deliver us!

A Scottish Presbyterian prayer

There was an eerie sound at the window, like a tree branch brushing against the glass pane. What was that sound? It's not pleasant being the only adult late at night in a houseful of helpless children, with a traveling husband far away.

Settling in with a really scary TV movie after the children were safely in bed wasn't my best idea. Now what? Were all the doors locked? Did that make much difference? With my fertile imagination, I thought of fifteen ways that the bad people could get in, and we'd only lived here three weeks.

It was dark, late, and windy on this lonely street where I didn't know my neighbors. Turning on lights and prowling the perimeter, I decided there were no bad guys. At least, not tonight.

What did I learn? For starters, don't watch scary movies alone just before bed. Even more valuable, I remembered my special nighttime psalm: "I will lie down and sleep in peace, for you alone, O Lord, make me dwell in safety" (Psalm 4:8).

But I cannot say that one experience ended suspicious nighttime noises and accompanying terrors. Over and over, my mind continued to generate what ifs regarding the dark, shadowy corners where quick escape would be difficult, or impossible. Read on and together let's explore how we may live free from fear of things that go bump in the night.

Twenty years ago I made a list of what I was afraid of:

I'm afraid

1. to be out of control.

2. to be unable to control the behavior of another.

3. to fail or make a mistake in front of certain people.

4. that my children may fail.

5. that my mouth will get me into trouble.

6. that I can't do something as well as those I admire.

7. that my shortcomings will become obvious.

8. that my children won't be happy.

9. that I, or my nearest and dearest, will fall ill and die young.

The common thread of most of these fears is that they are social fears, revolving around what people might think. My fears reflect what I most care about, what I love. Near and dear to me are my reputation, my comfort, and my family. Two questions haunt people at their core: "Will anybody love me?" and "Will I be capable of loving another?"

Frights from mice, spiders, and snakes pale before the icy fingers of fear that flood our veins when we hear that the diagnosis is a terminal disease. Our trepidation to drive on busy streets dims before the terror that wakes a single mother in the middle of the night as she wonders how she will raise the children alone, pay the bills, and put new shingles on the roof, while dodging the hostile behavior of an unkind ex-spouse. The alarm of things that go bump in the night fades against the terror that grips a parent who sees their child choose a life apart from God.

Anxiety attacks

Fear is the greatest challenge to overcome. Fear is very personal. It is not age specific. It affects children, teens, singles, marrieds, mothers, fathers, widows, widowers, and the elderly. It determines who we are, what we do, and where we go. Everything.

The Greek word for fear is *phobos*, meaning flight, panic, and terror. It is the origin for our common word, phobia. The *New Webster's Dictionary* defines fear as "anxiety caused by expectation of evil, danger; awe; dread". Anxiety is a tearing apart. The degree of fear can range from feeling anxious about a new situation, to panic that causes physical tremors, cold sweat, and heart palpitations. Prolonged fear can cause ulcers, weight loss (not a recommended plan!), loss of sleep, and panic attacks. Abnormal, consistent fears or phobias can cripple, suffocate, and strangle a productive life. In the case of agoraphobia, fear of leaving one's own home chokes the potential right out of a person.

Someone gave the fear factor this acronym:

False

Evidence

Appearing

Real

Our most common fears express themselves in our everyday language. "This is going to be the death of me" is a phrase we banter about. Probably it isn't, but the wording may gain someone's attention. To add seriousness to a subject, we say we are scared to death when we don't really mean it.

Yet, each of us can name something that scares us to death. Would you rather die than speak in front of people? There is the memory of standing there paralyzed as your mind goes blank. The time seemed endless. Actually it was probably more like seconds. At its core, that is a fear of rejection or failure. Fear of speaking in front of others has fallen to second place behind the fear of not having enough money for retirement. Remember Y2K? We wrote, worried, prepared, and strategized. And as you remember, it never happened. Though the list is always in flux, today's newspaper reflects the fears that dog contemporary society:

- The skin cancer threat.

- Media coverage – is it biased or not?

- Terrorist attacks.

- The loss of civility and common courtesy.

- The demise of patriotism and the lack of leaders.

- What if my body outlives my mind?

- Will Social Security and Medicare fail?

Mothers worry about their children even after they're grown and have independent lives of their own. And who doesn't worry about what the medical test results will say regarding our health or the health of a loved one? Chronic or terminal illness shatters our belief that we are in control of our own life. It reminds us that we are mortal.

Since I was a little girl, I have feared cancer. I had

the impression that if you get it, you die. Too often that is still true. Dementia and Alzheimer's are scary. We fear losing who we are, and our lives shrinking and shrinking into nothingness. My darling 81-year-old neighbor comes to my home and I fix tea. We sit on the porch and I hug her while she cries. "I just can't remember things," she tells me. "I don't know where my mind is going."

What we know

A less than blessed attribute of our modern society is that we know too much. Or we think we do. I've read about diseases I've never imagined, percentages of risk for household accidents, car accidents, bike accidents, and hiking accidents. There are mortality tables for those who smoke, drink, don't exercise, use salt, eat fat, or don't eat fat. A recent report said strokes occur most often on Mondays. Now I'm afraid of Mondays.

Media overload contributes to our fear. Our Sunday newspaper holds more news than a person living 200 years ago received in a year or maybe a lifetime. Reports about terrorism, wars, abuse, and crime cause us to fear that something terrible might happen to us. And the scientific findings constantly change. One woman who regularly goes to lunch with a group of friends opens her menu each time and asks, "What doesn't cause cancer this week?"

Ignorance can be frightening. Not knowing how to tackle a challenge, how to approach a difficult person, or what will happen next. When Luis and I served as missionaries in Colombia, I met a young woman who feared the coming of a second child because she was certain that she had caused the death of her first. She simply lacked basic information regarding the childbirth process. I was able to explain why the first birth had not had a successful outcome, and impart healthy hope for her future as a mother.

Our temperament affects our propensity to worry. Some folks are born worry warts. One elderly lady who had worried all her life, used to say if she gave up worrying, she wouldn't be good at anything. Some fears are learned. Our grandmother and mother before us may have been frightened of flying or some such concern and that fear may have been taught to us. Mothers who are fearful of water find it hard to let their children play near it, or even learn to swim. I ask them, "Was your mother afraid of water?"

While we have eliminated some of our foremothers' top fears either through the curing of a dreaded childhood disease such as polio, or enlightened information that our great dreaded fear never existed in the first place, new modern fears have quickly stepped into the vacuum. In my childhood, we observed summertime restrictions about public places where polio might lurk. Today we have substituted new afflictions such as autism, depression, and other poorly understood maladies.

Toxic relationships

Perhaps you've been wounded or betrayed, hurt or abused. Negative past experiences can cause us to fear people, situations, or the future. Those who have been betrayed are frequently afraid of rejection. They see themselves as not worthy and valueless, all the while fearful that others see them in the same light. Their intense fear of abandonment is housed in neediness, in a loss of self from striving to be what they perceive another person wants. The fear of loneliness and rejection is so intense that people remain in toxic relationships, driven by their core belief that a bad relationship is better than none at all.

I have spent almost as much of my married life by myself as with my husband, because he travels in ministry. I am not afraid of things that go bump in the night. I am not afraid of the dark and if my children don't telephone and remind me, I rarely remember to shut the doors, let alone lock them.

But I am scared of some things. Especially snakes. It goes back to the Garden of Eden. When God was calling me as a young single woman to go to the mission field, don't think that I didn't get out the encyclopedia and look up all the places that don't have snakes.

I'm not alone in my fear of snakes. My friend shares my dread of these reptiles. She says, "Once, in a movie theatre, a preview showed a snake slithering down a tree with an unsuspecting heroine underneath. I screamed so loud, the person behind me tapped my shoulder and said, 'Lady, please don't do that. I have a bad heart!' To this day, I tread carefully in high grass. I am a chicken when it comes to snakes."

I have a terror of unemployment which comes from nowhere. It is irrational. I lack faith that I, or anyone near and dear to me, could ever get a job. Jobs and their accompanying paychecks represent security. Whatever my problem, can I throw money at it? Someone said that money isn't everything, but it sure calms my nerves. We fear the loss of security and are intimidated by bosses who hold our future employment in their hands.

There are fears that require the Word of God in the hands of a specialized helper. When a fear is deeply rooted, interrupting life, and damaging those we love, then it is time to seek help from a godly, trained counselor. During therapy, it is vital to be diligent in your recovery work. They don't call it work for nothing – it is serious business.

Most of what we deal with as human beings is what the Bible terms "such as is common to man." In other words, very real, very scary, and very ordinary. I want to live a life not characterized by a worried look. There are laugh lines and there are worry lines. I don't aspire to resemble Winnie the Pooh's friend, Eeyore. It's cute on a stuffed donkey, but not when it's me!

All of us are in process when it comes to self-confidence and courage to follow Christ. I am encouraged by the time-element evident in the Apostle Paul's statement, "And I am convinced and sure of this very thing, that he who began a good work in you will continue until the day of Jesus Christ [right up to the time of his return], developing [that good work] and perfecting and bringing it to full completion in you" (Philippians 1:6, Amplified). There is great encouragement to all us cowardly lions who wish to face our fears in a Christ-honoring way, but fall short of our own ideals. In this verse is certainty – we can be sure. There is a sense of history – a sense of who is doing the work. And there is more assurance – he will continue his work until it is finished. In this verse is an ultimate outcome – when Christ Jesus returns.

What do you fear?

"Do not be afraid," Jesus Christ said. He said that to every group he talked to. We are all afraid. But we are also in the process of living a fearless life. God's Word to us – his instruction, "do not fear" – is spoken to us today every bit as much as it was spoken to the people of the Old and New Testaments in our Bible. Certainly we are unique, but human nature is the same today as it was thousands of years ago. That is why God and his living Word are relevant to you and me today.

What is the thing that you fear? What are the situations that you don't trust the Lord with? We're all pretty much alike, though where we focus our worries may be different. Our circumstances are not the source of our security and peace. When something goes bump in the night, we need to remember that "God did not give us a spirit of timidity, but a spirit of power, of love and of self-discipline" (2 Timothy 1:7).

Fears begin as solitary units, one at a time, but then they reproduce, multiply, and gang up on us. That's stress. The relatives of fearful situations are hypothetical "what ifs," wondering, guessing, and presumptions. We word these in terms of something that might, could, or will possibly happen. One day when my 17-year-old son went out, I was sure he was up to mischief. Secretly, I followed his car. Sure enough, the car parked in a shady parking lot and someone came to the driver's window. After some conversation, the car proceeded to another location. That's when the driver got out and I realized I'd been following the wrong vehicle. That night, my son was exactly where he was supposed to be. I had projected suspicions and fears about where he was and what he was doing.

Similarly, when one of my sons was 9, I noticed he was blinking a lot. He seemed twitchy. Immediately I projected the worst. When I asked my son about his behavior, he didn't provide a satisfying answer, so I took him to the doctor.

The doctor looked at me and asked, "Now, Mrs Palau, what was it that you brought him in for?"

"He's sort of... twitching," I answered. "I asked him why but he didn't know."

"Why did you ask him that? In his mind your child is trying to give you a good answer." The doctor instructed, "Never ask a child why. Ask him what."

I pressed on: "I was kind of thinking that it might be a brain tumor."

"Well, I wasn't." He then suggested that if his older

brothers would leave him alone, maybe he would quit twitching. Sometimes ignorance can cause fear. Too much information, or memories of things from the past can trigger worry. Our fears surface when we find we can't control our surroundings. Lack of control triggers our fear. Rather than trust God, we daily trust in the areas where we are strong. My two areas of strength were where God touched me. He gave me a child who was inscrutable to me. I ran out of ideas. He outfoxed me and all my child psychology techniques. Secondly, I thought my physical and mental health was something I could control. But when I had cancer, the idea that I could just "buck up" no longer worked. Clarity was replaced by confusion, an inability to make decisions.

Without fearsome situations, those circumstances that are out of our control, we would not rely on God. Some people are obsessively fearful. The Bible tells us not to preview the future. "Therefore do not worry about tomorrow, for tomorrow will worry about itself. Each day has enough trouble of its own" (Matthew 6:34).

I lift up my eyes to the hills –
where does my help come from?
My help comes from the Lord,
the Maker of Heaven and earth.
He will not let your foot slip –
he who watches over you will not slumber;
indeed, he who watches over Israel
Will neither slumber nor sleep.
The Lord watches over you –

the Lord is your shade at your right hand;
the sun will not harm you by day,
nor the moon by night.
The Lord will keep you from all harm –
he will watch over your life;
the Lord will watch over your coming and going
both now and forevermore.

PSALM 121

APPLICATION POINT

1. What scares you to death? Why does this fear outrank all other fears?

2. What is the thing that you don't trust the Lord with?

STEPPING OUT

Now, as you begin to read, I have just one more suggestion. Do not – I repeat, do not – skip over the Scripture verses included in this book. They are meant to be read – that's why they are printed out. They are unique. They are God's thoughts on the subject at hand. There is really no particular reason why you should take my thoughts seriously, only as they reflect God's.

You may wonder why I mention this. I remember long ago in our missionary years, sitting with a friend while we evaluated a four-page Christian pamphlet, in those days called a tract. I was looking through it with my steel-trap mind, making sure that certain basic truths of the Good News were clear. Looking up, I noticed that my co-worker had already finished. "I just read the story parts," she admitted. "I skipped over the Scriptures."

Don't do that! Stories and illustrations are just that – the writer's efforts to clarify and solidify the gospel truth about our subject, fear.

I admit that it is common practice to presume that we already know the noted Scripture verses. There are lots of kinds of *know*. If we already truly applied what the Bible says on the subject of fear, you would never have picked up this book. And, I would not have written it.

When we have been followers of Christ for a long time, we tend to pass right over the familiar. The truth is located somewhere in our minds, but has not yet impacted our lives or affected our hearts. Ask God, the Holy Spirit, to open your heart and mind to the reality of truths not fully applied. "The unfolding of your words gives light; it gives understanding to the simple" (Psalm 119:130).

Ask the Lord to make the words living and applicable, as if you were seeing them for the first time. The One who brings life to the words on the page indwells us and empowers us to obey and change.

There are no short-cuts to conquering our fears. There is, though, the all-knowing, all-caring One who lives within us and his most comforting word, *Fear not!*

CHAPTER 2

THE FEARS WE NEED

The fear of the Lord is the beginning of knowledge,
but fools despise wisdom and discipline.

PROVERBS 1:7

If you know with certainty that God loves you and
that He desires good for you,
What is there to fear? What is there to dread? What
is there to be depressed about?
I am not making light of fears, doubts, or depression.
They are normal human responses.
Hope, however, compels you not to remain in a state
of fear, doubt, or depression.
Hope encourages you to raise your eyes and look for
the dawn of a new day.
Hope calls you to anticipate God's best.

CHARLES STANLEY, *THE REASON FOR MY HOPE*

Are there things that we should be afraid of? Things
that we ought to fear?

There are three kinds of fear: slavish fears or

phobias; self-preserving fears; and the holy fear of God.

"Do not be afraid of those who kill the body but cannot kill the soul. Rather, be afraid of the One who can destroy both soul and body in hell" (Matthew 10:28). The fear of God is an awesome reverence. "His pleasure is not in the strength of the horse, nor his delight in the legs of a man; the Lord delights in those who fear him, who put their hope in his unfailing love" (Psalm 147:10–11).

To fear God is to be awed by him, and to have a deep desire not to offend him. The result is a healthy urge toward obedience. When we possess a healthy fear of God, it helps us understand his love for us, increases our trust in him, and we begin to eliminate our anxious fears.

> *We know that we live in him and he in us, because he has given us of his Spirit. And we have seen and testify that the Father has sent his Son to be the Savior of the world. If anyone acknowledges that Jesus is the Son of God, God lives in him and he in God. And so we know and rely on the love God has for us. God is love. Whoever lives in love lives in God, and God in him. In this way, love is made complete among us so that we will have confidence on the day of judgment, because in this world we are like him. There is no fear in love. But perfect love drives out fear, because fear has to do with punishment. The one who fears is not made perfect in love. We love because he first loved us.*
>
> 1 JOHN 4:13–19

When we talk about the *fear of God* we run two risks: too much or too little. Isn't that life? We'll never achieve perfect balance while we live on this unbalanced, out-of-whack planet. That's what heaven's for. Today, we either water down the fear of God until it just means a polite acknowledgment, or we envision an angry God counting up points against us so that he can mete out an exact punishment. Moses understood the two types of fear when he told the people, "Do not be afraid. God has come to test you, so that the fear of God will be with you to keep you from sinning" (Exodus 20:20).

In the book of Acts, the church "was strengthened; and encouraged by the Holy Spirit, it grew in numbers, living in the fear of the Lord" (Acts 9:31). Fear of God, added to respect and a healthy amount of awe and even trembling, in the face of God's overwhelming power, leaves us just about where the biblical writers thought we should be. If we have just such a proper honor, it might change our behavior for the better. We've said nothing about a sniveling, cowardly, nail-biting terror. We have simply seen God's authentic power revealed in his Word, and then had it reaffirmed in the drama of nature, volcanoes, storms, and the roar of Niagara's waters.

When he talks, however we hear him, we should listen. That's a healthy fear of God.

My fear shows what, or who, I trust. Instinct prompts me to run and hide from what I fear. It is a natural reaction to try to control circumstances and the environment so I avoid what I fear. At first glance, it seems easier to avoid the threat rather than face it and take it to the Lord. Controlling people are fearful people. What we work overtime to control illuminates what we find most fearsome.

Shadrach, Meshach, and Abednego feared God more than they feared the most fearsome and unpredictable ruler of their day. When they wouldn't worship King Nebuchadnezzar's statue, these Hebrew captives turned king's staff were threatened with capital punishment.

"O Nebuchadnezzar," they said, "we do not need to defend ourselves before you in this matter. If we are thrown into the blazing furnace, the God we serve is able to save us from it, and he will rescue us from your hand, O king. But even if he does not, we want you to know, O king, that we will not serve your gods or worship the image of gold you have set up" (Daniel 3:16–18).

Pressured to compromise their faith, these men wouldn't bend or bow. They'd rather burn. Though the king had the fire stoked ten times hotter just for them, the three revered God more than they feared being thrown into a fiery furnace. "The king's command was so urgent and the furnace so hot that the flames of the fire killed the soldiers who took up Shadrach, Meshach and Abednego, and these three men, firmly tied, fell into the blazing furnace" (Daniel 3:22–23).

When the three chose the fear of the Lord over the fear of the fire, they not only didn't burn, but the Lord met them inside the furnace. King Nebby declared, "Look! I see four men walking around in the fire, unbound and unharmed, and the fourth looks like a son of the gods" (Daniel 3:25).

Shadrach, Meshach, and Abednego exemplified a holy fear of the holy God and the only thing that burned was the ropes that bound them.

Holy fear

What fire are you going through? When we face our own fiery furnace, can you and I choose to fear God more than we fear the flames? It is easier said than done. Sometimes, like the account in the book of Daniel, there is a miracle. Sometimes God allows us to suffer. Sometimes he allows us to die. Sometimes the greater miracle is not that God rescues us from the fire, but that he is with us through it.

Corrie ten Boom's family members risked their own lives to save Jewish people from the horrors of the Holocaust. Then Corrie and her loved ones were arrested and subjected to the very evils they were trying to preserve others from. Corrie alone survived. The ordeal, the sacrifice they invested, cost her sister and father their lives. Corrie did not come away unscathed. She experienced indescribable horrors inflicted on herself and her fellow prisoners.

Similarly, Dietrich Bonhoeffer, a German Christian pastor, was killed by the Nazis mere days before the Allied forces defeated the German war machine. But at all times God is with us. The Lord may use the fire to refine us.

"Even though I walk through the valley of the shadow of death, I will fear no evil, for you are with me" (Psalm 23:4). We may have to walk through the valley of the shadow of death. But he will never leave us alone. Ultimately he will reward us. God is more interested in the development of our character and spiritual growth, than he is in rescuing you and me from circumstances that make us uncomfortable and fearful. Do you think Shadrach, Meshach, and Abednego were afraid of being thrown into the flames? I have no doubt that they were scared to death. What makes them heroes is not an absence of fear. They are heroes to all generations because they chose God over and above their fear.

Today, we are constantly pressured to bow down to the gods of this world. The majority of people will yield. We justify giving in to our fears with thin excuses such as, "Everyone else is doing it," and "I don't really mean it in my heart," and "As long as it doesn't hurt anyone else, what does it matter?"

Anytime we place something ahead of God in our lives, that something or someone becomes an idol. God is replaced on the throne of our hearts with cheap imitations such as pleasure, power, pride, or materialism. The more we understand what God is like, the clearer we are about ourselves, our souls, our humanity, and our failure compared to the attributes of God and his high standards. That kind of fear is a holy fear.

"Therefore, there is now no condemnation for those who are in Christ Jesus, because through Christ Jesus the law of the Spirit of life set me free from the law of sin and death" (Romans 8:1).

Nature or nurture

There is a self-preservation kind of fear where you say, "Only an idiot would not be afraid of…"

One afternoon there was a knock at my door and a man was standing on my doorstep. "Ladies, I don't want to scare you," he said, "but there is a child walking up on the roof peak line."

Well, I knew which child that was, so I went outside and told him, "You get down from there right now!" But that's how that child was. He was born reckless. He didn't have the natural fear he should have had about walking on the roof peak line.

Some children are born with an extra spark plug while others are born tentative, thinking, and cautious. One of our premature twin baby boys cried desperately at the bass sound of a wonderful missionary friend's voice. From his earliest days he was terrified of the deep masculine voice. That's nature. My grandmother was scared of snakes and she taught that to my mother, who taught me to be afraid of snakes. That's nurture.

Attaching a fear to the next person, the next relationship, passing values from parents to relatives and spouses is nurture. Sometimes people are… well… people. We tell ourselves lies; that we are not enough for that person, incapable of making the relationship work, unable to handle a project God has called us to. Those lies can be passed to the next generation or we can make a conscious decision to stop the pattern and raise our children to be confident and secure in our love, in themselves, and in the unconditional love and equipping of God.

We nurture and coddle pet fears. Those are recognized by the excuses we attach to them: "Well, I always feel this way," or "I can never find victory in this area." Some fears are inconvenient, but clever people find ways to disguise the true diagnosis with, "I'm not fearful, just careful." It's just so much easier than being honest. Interestingly, we are the only ones who believe our excuses. Everyone else sees right through them.

One friend prefers not to fly on airplanes. I don't give a thought to how far above ground I am. However, now and again she serves as my chauffeur and drives me across the Willamette River into what I call unfamiliar territory. We both *could* manage these trips, if we had to, but prefer to find a way of escape. We weigh our fears and decide not to face them. At least not right now.

First lessons

We all learn to be afraid of touching a hot stove. We teach our children to be scared of crossing a busy street without first looking to be sure the way is safe. That's what I love about toddlers. They love life, giggle plenty, and fear nothing. It's sad that one of our responsibilities is to make them aware of life-threatening dangers that lie just beyond their pudgy little feet.

Often children are frightened by what they don't know. We comfort small children with the assurance that they are perfectly safe in our care. No, there are no monsters in the closet nor under the bed. Mothers often fall asleep beside a fearful child with an overactive imagination.

The other day I read one of the Berenstain Bears books to three-year-old Luke. He picks his favorites, after he's heard them about fifteen times. This one had to do with a scary noise in the night which turned out to be the wind in the trees. The solution was a night light that Papa Bear got down from the attic. He'd saved it from his childhood, implying that he too was afraid of the dark as a youngster.

The theme of children's books is usually that something looks scary, imagination takes over, closets are checked by patient daddies and mommies and sure enough, there's nothing there. Things are not as they fear and in the light of day, or with a good night light, the child or baby bear is no longer scared to death.

Parents have a major task unmasking scary concepts, mostly imaginary and arising right around bedtime. Some fears come from the teasing of older siblings. The fear may be real and could be caught from a parent. The dentist, people in white coats bearing needles, things like that. Some things are scary. We have to be sure that we are displaying a healthy confidence in God's providence and a willingness to discuss in an age-appropriate way how we have learned to trust, and not be afraid.

There is nothing worse than lying to a child – "It won't hurt," when you know it will. Just as the greatest help we have is the promise of God's presence, so also the confidence we show our children, that they are in safe hands, ours and God's, helps them develop a coping strategy for the truly scary things of life.

We have a responsibility to take the words *age appropriate* very seriously. Children slip into their parents' bedroom in the middle of the night with a bad dream that arose out of an inappropriately scary image they viewed on television. Although the direct issue may be dealt with and dismissed, the frightening picture may plant itself in the recesses of a child's mind. For a lifetime. I have vague memories of stories I read in the newspaper when I was seven years old. I was quite proud of myself that I could read the paper, but some of the news items were not at all appropriate. And that was before television.

All of Psalm 119 shows the benefit of allegiance to God and knowledge of his Word. We benefit from a holy fear of disobeying the Lord God Almighty. "I have set before you life and death, blessings and curses. Now choose life, so that you and your children may live and that you may love the Lord your God, listen to his voice, and hold fast to him" (Deuteronomy 30:19–20). God has provided instructions for life in his Word. The Ten Commandments tell us what to do and what not to do. We benefit from having a holy fear of disobeying the Lord God Almighty who created heaven and earth:

You shall have no other gods before me.

EXODUS 20:3

Come, my children, listen to me;
I will teach you the fear of the Lord.

PSALM 34:11

The self-preservation fear has been hard-wired into us by our Creator. It is the healthy fear of touching a fire, or gripping an electric wire. It guides us to make wise choices regarding obeying traffic laws and caring for our bodies. Our medical community is flourishing because we want good health. In the present generation, we began practicing preventative medicine. That means we do regular testing on our bodies to prevent disease or to catch it in the early stages and eradicate it before the illness becomes life-threatening.

First fears

Biologists tell us that fear is not only a universal emotion but the first of the emotions to be developed in both the human and animal kingdoms. The whole creation is under the control and domination of fear. Babies are born into a world already stamped by fear. These fears increase as the child grows both physically and emotionally.

Have you ever picked up a baby bird and felt its frantically beating heart? The poor little bird has had no experience with you or any other human. It has no reason to fear you other than pure instinct. It is in dread of everything but its mother and its siblings. Looking at the world around us, perhaps this instinctual fear is a necessary evil.

47

The pace of our lives continues to get busier, and the resulting stress is a constant companion and the breeding-ground for all types of physical illness. There are very few blank squares in my calendar. Despite my seven decades, I think my memory is fine. Luis tells me he told me something, but I actually don't think he did. He's the one who forgot.

Fear can't face truth. It does not help to minimize danger and possible outcomes. Fear thrives on vague and inaccurate information. In the midst of busy schedules and changing circumstances, we mature in our relationship with our God. While some of our anxieties originate from our own inner thoughts, some are thrown at us by Satan, the enemy of our souls.

Determining the source helps determine the response. Is the problem or issue clear? If it is a vague, indefinable cloud that floats over my head, characterized by a general uneasiness, that points to an evilness. In these instances, speak aloud: "Satan, get out of here. I have nothing to do with you. I belong to Christ." Martin Luther did this.

Satan accuses. The Holy Spirit convicts clearly. God speaks plainly to get our attention, warn us, and urge us to act. Life as a Christian is not a game. God treats us as his beloved children. Our heavenly Father does not taunt or frustrate us.

Holy fear motivates us to positive action. It is guilt-free. Holy fear encourages self-preservation, care of the creation, and good stewardship of what God has graciously placed in our hands. "See if you can figure this out," we imagine God saying. That will never happen. God wants us to understand. He wants us to have a sound mind. Often we are afraid to step out, sometimes to obey God. We resist taking a risk lest we fail. Failure is human. It is not sin. Failure is often an excellent teacher. ✗

While phobias are slavish and suffocating, the self-preservation fear of touching a hot stove and the holy fear and respect of our righteous God are life-giving attitudes.

> *Do not be afraid, for I have ransomed you. I have called you by name, you are mine. When you go through deep waters and great trouble I will be with you. When you go through rivers of difficulty, you will not drown. When you walk through the fire of oppression, the flames will not consume you. I am your Savior.*
>
> ISAIAH 43:1–3 (NEW LIVING TRANSLATION)

APPLICATION POINT

1. "If you love me, you'll obey what I command," the Lord directs (John 14:15). A good place to begin is with the Ten Commandments (Exodus 20:3–17).

2. Fear strangles our creativity. Yet God created you with talents and abilities. We are most like Christ when we forgive and when we create. Cultivate creativity in your life. For me, that means gardening and knitting. Rest in the Lord as you create something new and beautiful.

STEPPING OUT

I know a pastor who, when he suspects that something in his life is becoming more important than God, gives up that thing for one day each week to be sure that he rules his flesh, rather than his flesh ruling him. Some of us make idols of shopping, eating, drinking, computer time, sleeping, movies, or music. Offer that time to the Lord one day per week.

CHAPTER 3

THE FEAR OF MAN

Fear of man will prove to be a snare
But whoever trusts in the Lord is kept safe.

PROVERBS 29:25

Besides looking for a country that didn't have snakes,
I did a lot of silly, useless exercises of my heart and
soul preparing for what I thought I would face as a
missionary. They never happened. I never experienced
any of it. I never let fears or phobias affect my time
on the mission field. But I did experience other things
that I should have been better prepared for. And it
often centered around the fear of man.

We experience fear dealing with others because
the stakes seem disproportionately high. Problems
getting along with people, at their worst, result in
broken relationships, divorce, and divided churches
and organizations. On a larger scale, problems getting
along with other people lead to war. No wonder we
tip-toe around volatile people in hopes of maintaining
the status quo, in hopes of keeping peace.

The most stressful problem in life is the same one in every setting and in every era. It is the same issue that I faced on the mission field and that I face today. Leading to relationship break-ups on small and large scales, the most stressful problem in missionary work is not snakes, the environment, or exotic diseases. The thing that causes the most stress and anxiety centers around getting along with other people. The fancy term is "interpersonal relationships". It is often why missionaries come home. And that's what drives me to my knees whether I live overseas or in my hometown.

The fear of man is prevalent in the church and Christian culture where we've developed habit patterns that are perceived as virtues. When we speak a common language differently, misunderstanding comes easily.

Biblically, the fear of man is rooted in cowardice. I have thought and thought, trying to find an updated, modern term for the biblical words, *fear of man*. The biblical term 'man' is generic for the human species, both male and female. I wish there were another phrase. "Fear of people" would be more accurate but, alas, it is awkward. Maybe "excessive people-pleasing" might work. "Co-dependency." "Peer pressure."

Balance is key to everything. There is a normal, healthy desire in all of us to make others happy. Go along to get along. However, in the extreme, people-pleasing becomes an obsession. The line is crossed when we deny our own knowledge of the Truth, our Holy Spirit-driven conscience, to achieve or remain in the good graces of those we perceive to be our betters. There! That's a definition. Through practice we develop coping mechanisms. We may run like a deer, hold our ground, or make distracting excuses.

At its core, people-pleasing is idolatry. When I care more about what others may think than I do about what God thinks, I have placed people above God. "You shall have no other gods before me," the Lord declares in Exodus 20:3. Years later I look back and wonder how I could have let that happen.

The high cost we pay

King Solomon said, "The fear of man brings a snare." A snare is a trap. No one deliberately falls into a trap. Yet being controlled by fear is enslaving. It is a snare.

- Snares have a degree of attraction.

- They slow us down.

- They distract us from our God-given purpose.

- Over time, they cause a sense of helplessness and insecurity.

The fear of man, what others think of us, is a most pervasive fear. We fear rejection, abandonment, betrayal, loneliness. These fears cause us to compromise healthy relationship boundaries, and sacrifice principles. This fear causes people to remain in unhealthy relationships or to repeat them.

One woman gave in to sex before marriage to

prove her love to her boyfriend. When a pregnancy resulted, she gave in to an abortion so she wouldn't lose him. When he wasn't faithful, she tried to be thinner and more available so he wouldn't have reason to stray. This noxious cycle continued because she was more concerned about pleasing a man than about pleasing the Lord.

A Supreme Court justice once said that he could not define pornography, but knew it when he saw it. I feel the same about the fear of man. It's difficult to articulate this fear of other people, but so many of the major hang-ups, fears, and roadblocks I've had to work through lie in this area.

For instance, I was with a group of women and the subject of a highly acclaimed movie came up. Everyone extolled its impact, beauty, and merit. Though the movie featured suicide, various kinds of sexual perversions, and child neglect, I didn't speak up. I was afraid of being viewed as naïve, fundamentalist, and simplistic. Knowing someone I admired held a diametrically opposed point of view, I modified my statements. I compromised, looking instead for common ground we could agree on. While that may sometimes be the logical approach, in that moment, what those individuals thought was more important to me than what God thinks. "Cursed is the one who trusts in man, who depends on flesh for his strength and whose heart turns away from the Lord" (Jeremiah 17:5).

But this fear of man isn't a problem I suffer with only around the general public. At a gathering of fellow Christians, I was on my best behavior and hoping the group would notice how smart I am. When the conversation drifted to contemporary issues, I didn't voice my opinion. Though based on Scripture, I knew my old-fashioned opinion was out of sync with societal trends. I kept my mouth shut.

Keeping my mouth shut may often be a good idea. But the motive was not. The truth is that I care tremendously about what certain people will think of me. This fear is often focused on educational levels. I fear to speak my mind before people whose educational level is higher than mine. I fear mockery and potential rejection. Will they roll their eyes behind my back? They use words I don't quite understand but I won't ask for clarification. I orchestrate my remarks to build up their estimation of me. My fear motivates me to manipulate.

When I am honest, I can encourage others. A popular television host once recommended a book that our contemporary culture embraced. When a friend asked my opinion, I told her why, biblically, the book was evil.

"That's what I wondered about," she said. "I felt it wasn't right." My confirmation echoed what God was already nudging in her spirit.

Family fears

Fear of man can have its strongest hold in family settings. Many grown children make decisions that they know are wrong based on a desire to please a parent. Too many parents offer acceptance conditioned on whether the child does what the parent wants. The source of the handicapping fear that hinders us from living life, following our dreams, and exercising our God-given talents often lives in our own household.

My high-school friend had three passions – the Lord, friends, and books. Her aspiration was to get a degree in librarianship. Years later, we crossed paths again, except now she was frustrated and unfulfilled among a pile of shattered dreams. Her father was a tough and volatile man who I remember giving a wide berth. Adamant that he wasn't going to spend hard-earned money to educate a girl to do something that didn't pay well, he coerced my friend into a career in medicine.

Though her father had been dead for years, this adult daughter hadn't broken free from his selfish, controlling dominion. Being middle-aged added to her fear about following her ambitions. I encouraged her to return to her early dreams.

Grandparents, in-laws, siblings, spouses, and other extended family can be a source of fear when displeasing that person results in punishments ranging from mockery to rejection. Individuals live in a sibling's shadow, crippled by unwise comments made by relatives or teachers during childhood. These wounds create a generalized tendency to flee from people and opportunity.

According to the biblical account, through the deceit of her father, Leah shared her husband with her younger and more beautiful sister Rachel. Jacob loved Rachel and despised the love-sick Leah. Because

Rachel was infertile, Leah traded "love apples" or mandrakes, thought to promote conception, for a night with Jacob. "You must come into me, for I have surely hired you with my son's mandrakes," Leah told Jacob that night when he came in from the fields.

Like Leah, who found herself bartering mandrake roots for sex because she was rejected by her husband (Genesis 30:14–16), too many women seek counseling where they confess they never dreamed they would be doing what they are involved in. Jill Briscoe writes: "They say, 'I can't believe I'm doing what I'm doing. But that's what he's asking me to do. Maybe then he'll love me.'" Fear of rejection drives women to do things that they don't feel very good about themselves for doing.

When I choose to jump through all kinds of unhealthy hoops for supervisors, bosses, teachers, pastors, and other authority figures, I make my life miserable. These phantom figures may have no intent to influence, but it is real to me and I'm inclined to act on it. I attempt the impossible effort to please the unpleasable. The fear of man is a habit that molds our lives. Fear often originates from those closest to us. It is often a family project. Whether it's real or imagined makes no difference.

Luis confronts the temptation to soften biblical teaching regarding sin in order to supposedly find more open doors for the message of the gospel. Sin can be called weakness, failure, anything that diminishes responsibility. The fine line lies between the desire to keep the door open to tell all people about Christ, and denying the person and work of Jesus Christ. This is an era of political correctness and tolerance. Tolerance for all other belief systems except the Good News of Jesus Christ.

Tolerance is rooted in the word "tolerate." To me, it means I am respectful of a person. Modern society translates "tolerance" to mean I must *accept* what others believe. What it really means is that I respect your right to believe what you choose. It does not mean I must hold all views of equal value.

During the promotion for a city-wide Festival of Good News, the local paper carried a story about a professional athlete who was to give his testimony as part of the event. A sophisticated, worldly-wise reporter trapped the young athlete into a statement that a former girlfriend was not a suitable life partner because she was not a professing Christian. The athlete was roundly criticized for his remarks, but I thanked God that this young man spoke truth that was not politically correct in a day of relativism.

As an evangelist first in Latin America, and now all over the world including the United States, Luis refers to this verse by the Apostle Paul: "Am I now trying to win the approval of men, or of God? Or am I trying to please men? If I were still trying to please men, I would not be a servant of Christ" (Galatians 1:10).

We must all ask ourselves, "Whose servant am I? Man's or God's?" In honest moments, the answer too often will reveal a deeper concern for what another person thinks than what God thinks. Do we bank on God being the more loving, compassionate, and forgiving of the two? Why should I care what a bunch of people I may never see again think of me? Why am I so concerned about what people who I will see again think of me?

It really doesn't matter what people think because they don't have a heaven or hell to send you to.

PASTOR LUTHER WHITFIELD

Where flattery gets you

Flattery gets you everywhere but you don't take a clear conscience with you. The fear of man hinders God's work in our lives. It hampers personal growth and maturity. It keeps us from positively impacting others. When we choose to please others at the cost of our standards and beliefs, we give up our genuine, vulnerable, authentic self. We trade the unique person God made each of us to be for a false self. When this behavior is habitual, we lose the sense of who we are in Christ. We become indecisive. "A double-minded man [or woman] is unstable in all his [or her] ways" (James 1:8, KJV). Why? Because we can't remember which side we're on and sometimes we try to be on all sides.

Fear of man is not only a contemporary problem. Abraham's fear of the Egyptians caused him to lie and to leave his wife unprotected. "Say you are my sister, so that I will be treated well for your sake and my life will be spared because of you," Abraham instructed

Sarai (Genesis 12:13). His fear for his own wellbeing prompted him to compromise his vows to his wife. Abraham's fear destroyed his opportunity to positively impact that pagan king.

Jesus daily dealt with the fear of man, confronting religious leaders. The atmosphere was such that the Pharisee Nicodemus, concerned about the reaction of his peers, came to see Jesus in the night (John 3:2). In John 9, Jesus created quite a stir when he healed the man born blind. The man's parents hedged in their reply when the Pharisees asked how their son was healed, because they were afraid of the religious leadership, for already they had decided that anyone who acknowledged that Jesus was the Christ would be put out of the synagogue (John 9:22). Powerbrokers and community leaders, the Pharisees held the key to the parents' public acceptance or rejection.

For us, as followers of Christ, the fear of man generally comes from traditions and legalisms within the church, doing extra-biblical practices rather than what God calls us to.

We all have people whose opinions mean a great deal to us. When I speak I tend to look over to see a certain person's response. When I was younger I was taught by a fantastic Bible teacher in our church. She had a steel-trap mind. I respected her – to a fault. The question in the back of my mind always was, "What will Mrs Fey think? Oh, I hope she's not here." Standing to speak and seeing her in the audience caused my heart to sink to my shoes. Certainly, to care what she thought was healthy, but to obsess over it was the fear of man (or woman!).

Fear of man includes an awe that is so excessive that it paralyzes us. It borders on idolatry. Observing the accomplishments or recognition or position or talents or the material wealth of others, we see ourselves as totally inferior. Our focus shifts off God's good gifts to us and his purposes for us. Instead, our vision is filled with where we sit in the hierarchy of totally superior individuals. This is false. It is a snare. A trap.

All of us have an inbred fear of those we perceive to be our betters. True leaders have overcome their fear of what other people think. They don't base decisions on focus groups, popular trends, or incessant polls. Basic principles and truths are their compass, and they adhere to an established philosophy of life. They are calm.

When I idolize or worship others, especially those I know only through the media, I deny God's redemptive work in my life. This creates a desire to look good in areas where I feel weak – the whole issue of image. Standing in someone's shadow appears safe, but it is the equivalent to burying our talent in the ground (Matthew 25:18). Your true self is made in the image of God. It takes an act of bravery to step out and be ourselves.

God has a unique purpose for each of us. Someone else's gift is not mine. I have no reason to compare myself negatively and shrink back from God's best gifts that he has placed in my hands.

People much more gifted than most of us will never stick out their necks to serve God because of a fear that someone, somewhere could do it better. I wrestle with this, too. I'm not the best *anything*, but if availability, and even foot-dragging reluctant willingness counts, then I have at least tried. The evangelist D. L. Moody once said, "I like the way I do it better than the way you don't."

Our fear and timidity toward people is often supreme. But the overwhelming truth is that as a child of God, I am indwelt by the Holy Spirit who delights to work through willing but weak children.

> *No one can make you feel inferior without your consent.*
>
> ELEANOR ROOSEVELT

Discouragement in the ranks

Fear of man breeds discouragement. In Numbers, the Israelites were afraid to go into the Promised Land because "All the people we saw there are of great size" (Numbers 13:32b).

Later, workers rebuilding Jerusalem's city walls found the surrounding peoples threatening and fearsome for good reason. "Then the peoples around them set out to discourage the people of Judah and make them afraid to go on building. They hired counselors to work against them and frustrate their plans during the entire reign of Cyrus king of Persia and down to the reign of Darius king of Persia" (Ezra 4:5).

Fear of man springs from our own insecurity. As in the case of the Israelites who were rebuilding the walls, sometimes our fear of man is born of the intentional meanness that others direct at us.

Ours is a success-driven society. We think bigger and better is best. We leave no place for reality. Our mantras are "I can do anything" and "I can achieve any goal my mind can conceive." Some years my work, output, and achievements are good. Other years are slower, uninspiring, and just don't work. I am not getting better and better day after day. I'm just more mature spiritually and closer to heaven. I am being conformed to the image of his Son. "For those God foreknew he also predestined to be conformed to the likeness of his Son, that he might be the firstborn among many brothers" (Romans 8:29).

Rather than being satisfied with the position where God placed us, and rejoicing in our relationship with him, we work harder. A church must grow numerically year after year. Otherwise, something is definitely wrong. Or is it? Today's workplace is cut-throat and runs counter to God's measurement for success. God calls us human beings. We push ourselves into human doings.

"Success is anything that pleases Him," said Henrietta Mears. What a relief to evaluate my workplace, career, and opportunities for growth without panic. To please only One. Positive thinking beats negative, untruthful talk. But somewhere in between is a biblical reality. I am a human and my desire is to please God with my life. Where my achievements land me is in his hands. My desire is that at the end of the day (I mean when it is all over and I've breathed my last), God might look at me and say something like, "Well done, good and faithful servant" (Matthew 25:23). That's an evaluation I can live with, without fear.

Years ago, I listed the three fears that tempted me to discouragement:

1. I can't do something well enough.

2. No one will like what I do.

3. I will fail and let down, or fail to impress, those I admire.

Not one word about cancer, or rebellious children. Pathetic concerns, actually, that I've since dealt with. But such is common to man. We all have common weaknesses that can be overcome by the indwelling of the Holy Spirit, who is committed to our success.

Why would anyone hang onto the fear of man and all its deceptiveness instead of trusting God? The habit begins in childhood. No one is totally fearful of all people at all times. Therefore it is easy to deceive myself by self-talk, emphasizing my limited exercises in courage. A few encounters where I represented the Savior bravely are overwhelmingly dominated by experiences denying the Son of God. Pure fear of man.

It's all about me

The fear of man is self-centered. It's all about me. It is impossible to focus on my fear, and how I am going to get through or around it, and at the same time demonstrate a healthy interest in the well-being of others.

Concern for what others may think of me puts me in a perpetual analytical pause. I question my abilities and do a lot of introspection. I spend money I shouldn't spend to buy clothes. I obsess over what I'm wearing when the fact is that I rarely notice what others are wearing and they don't notice what I'm wearing. I act on what I presume other people think. Why am I so self-focused, despite the fact that I profess to follow Christ? I am learning to resist that temptation.

The fear of man causes us to behave egotistically. Certainly there are times when we spot someone else trying to be what they are not. Name dropping, bragging, dressing and acting in an obviously self-serving manner. We all look pretty silly pontificating on subjects we know little about, pulling out our most aggressive body language to reinforce our position, or hiding in a corner practicing the art of becoming invisible.

Certain fears are life-long secrets. We don't say and no one can guess. Invisible to the world, we hide them. They don't show. Other fears are humiliating because they are so obvious. We often think we camouflage our fear of man with well-adapted people-pleasing behaviors. Even incredible humility. But those who are looking see the truth quickly. Our fear of man manifests in neediness, desperation, compromise, insincerity, making choices based on what we hope to manipulate from another. It might be favor, affection, or opportunity. It does not come from a place of authenticity and true grace. People instinctively don't like us. Life is short and we'd love to live surrounded by balanced, transparent, healthy people. I would love for people to think that I am candid, transparent, just myself as God's child. What you see is what you get.

Lives are ruined when we expend vast amounts of energy being what we are not. The world is desperately seeking those who will reach out to help. When they are asked what they want to do with their lives, most people say they want to help others. But giving is difficult when we are busy expending such effort and energy developing an image to peddle to the world. When my dream and idol is myself, struggling to maintain that elusive image leaves little room for unselfish service to a hurting humanity.

I could tell myself, when I get myself straightened out, I'll be a help to others. Fat chance! Feeding the insatiable ego is a full-time job and will never find completion.

When I was five years old, a man passed our house leading a pony. My mother asked if I wanted a ride. I panicked, embarrassed because I was afraid of the pony. My little brothers were jumping up and down, begging for a ride. "Let them," I hedged. "I have to wash the dishes." That was the first thought that popped into my mind and seemed a logical way to deal with the sticky matter of my fear of horses.

This episode was not so much about horses, but what the watching world would think about my clumsiness, lack of skills, and fear of horses.

I'm convinced that overcoming the fear of man is central to a believer's ability to grow up into a mature Christian. Not perfect, but moving forward.

The solution

We will never be free from the silly and sometimes serious handicaps of the fear of people, their opinions, or their hold over us until we face the basic fact that it is sin. Whether we call the fear a habit, a hang-up from childhood, or "just the way I am," it is failure to trust God and be honest.

All truth is good news and the good news about facing our fear of man is that this sin can be renounced and left behind. Murky tendencies and dysfunctions from the past are curable. If you struggle with long-standing sin, fears passed down from family members, it merely means you are in good company. The good news is that this can be the beginning of the end. Our great God loves you too much to leave you stuck.

The solution to the fear of man is simple, yet difficult to practice. The prescription is to over and over place the fear before the only critic whose opinion matters. If we seek to please the Lord, whose yoke is easy and whose burden is light (Matthew 11:28–30), the rest will fall into place. It is safest to be transparently honest because then I don't worry about what others will find out about me. I tell them about my struggles and my humanness.

Once and for all, we can hang up the chameleon suit we wore to be this for this person, and that for that person. "Love the Lord your God with all your heart and with all your soul, and with all your strength" (Deuteronomy 6:5).

To our heavenly Father, success lies in surrendering to a purpose that has eternal consequences and is worth the struggle. We must turn our eyes from our own achievements and those of others. Instead, focus on him. Work hard, set goals, and lean on the comfort of God's whisper, "I have loved you with an everlasting love, I have loved you with loving-kindness" (Jeremiah 31:3). The bottom line lies in whom we serve. Where is our heart? Who is keeping score?

I have been encouraged over the years by friends who looked at opportunities to progress in a corporate world, prayed, weighed their current situation, and decided to reject progress as the world sees it in favor of family welfare and spiritual security. Those decisions were long ago, yet looking back, God was faithful. Children grew up in a setting where family was known and roots went deep. In a generation of geographic upheaval, these families chose God's will.

When abandonment and rejection haunt you, remember that the only one who counts is the God who knows and loves you. He is the one who has engraved your name on his hand (Isaiah 49:16).

Make yourself accountable to someone you respect and begin the process of learning to trust in the Lord who has all that you need for success. When you are asked to do something, pray about it for twenty-four hours before responding. Regularly assess how you are progressing, recount your responses to people who intimidate you, and celebrate your growth.

There will be set-backs, of course. You are making progress as you recognize patterns and behaviors that used to automatically be your responses. You will cease to be a slave to any kind of fear, especially of the heavy-handed opinions of others. Your attitude will not be one of self-assertion, and pushiness, but of a forgiven child of God.

> *I pray that out of his glorious riches he may strengthen you with power through his Spirit in your inner being, so that Christ may dwell in your hearts through faith. And I pray that you, being rooted and established in love, may have power, together with all the saints, to grasp how wide and long and high and deep is the love of Christ, and to know this love that surpasses knowledge – that you may be filled to the measure of all the fullness of God.*
>
> EPHESIANS 3:16–19

For those of us who invested a long time repeating negative statements to ourselves, escaping from the fear of man and its reality of uselessness is a lot of work. A substantial amount of mental work landed us where we are today. The road to normalcy may appear long. But it's worth the struggle, for our own sakes, for our near and dear ones, and for the wider world who deal with us. To ask our fellow humans to devote their lives to figuring us out seems ultimately selfish. Particularly since God has offered us freedom from fear of man.

There is an old saying that appeared on wall

plaques: "Only one life, 'twil soon be past. Only what's done for Christ will last." Therefore, do your best, with eternity's values in view, and *fear not*.

> *The Lord is my light and my salvation –*
> *whom shall I fear?*
> *The Lord is the stronghold of my life –*
> *of whom shall I be afraid?*

PSALM 27:1

> *Do not fret because of evil men*
> *or be envious of those who do wrong;*
> *for like the grass they will soon wither,*
> *like green plants they will soon die away.*
> *Trust in the Lord and do good;*
> *dwell in the land and enjoy safe pasture.*
> *Delight yourself in the Lord*
> *and he will give you the desires of your heart.*

PSALM 37:1–4

APPLICATION POINT

1. Recall your most embarrassing moment. Who were you trying to please or impress in that instance?

2. Do you care deeply about what some people think of you? Who are they?

3. Are you concerned about how a group or organization views you?

4. Do these concerns about people and organizations supersede your concern for what God thinks?

STEPPING OUT

One day at a time, practice playing only to an audience of One. Give yourself the freedom to be genuine to yourself, to others, and to God.

Give your children worthy models. Read aloud books by Irene Hoyat, including *Ten Boys Who Changed the World, Ten Girls Who Changed the World, Ten Girls Who Made A Difference, Ten Boys Who Made A Difference,* and *Ten Girls Who Made History.*

Chapter 4

Don't Worry, Be Happy

Blessed is he whose help is the God of Jacob,
whose hope is in the Lord his God,
the Maker of Heaven and earth,
the sea, and everything in them –
the Lord who remains faithful forever.
He upholds the cause of the oppressed
and gives food to the hungry.
The Lord sets prisoners free,
the Lord gives sight to the blind,
the Lord lifts up those who are bowed down,
the Lord loves the righteous.
The Lord watches over the alien
and sustains the fatherless and the widow,
but he frustrates the ways of the wicked.

PSALM 146:5–9

I've suffered a great many catastrophes in my
life. Most of them never happened.

MARK TWAIN

I don't worry. I get peeved. I get stressed. I am often concerned. I feel anxious, and fearful. The rest of you worry and that is a sin. I just have serious concerns about things. (I hope you see the truth behind the sarcasm.)

We are the only species that worries. Worry by any other name is still a destructive habit. Worry is fear in action. Deceptive and unreasonable, all the worry in the world doesn't sharpen a pilot's skills or destroy cancer cells. An issue of trust, worry is a sin because it says, *God can't help me. I have to do this by myself. I have no one else to turn to. I have to be self-reliant.* Oswald Chambers said, "It is not only wrong to worry, it is unbelief; worrying means we do not believe that God can look after the practical details of our lives, and it is never anything but those details that worry us."

Jesus occasionally employed sarcasm to make the point. "Can all your worries add a single moment to your life?" (Matthew 6:27, NLT). Two things break fellowship between us and our Lord – sin and cares. Sin demands confession. Cares, or worry, demand that we leave our burdens with him.

We can't flourish if we combine work with worry. Worry accomplishes nothing except to rob our minds of possible solutions. I usually worry about the uncontrollable behavior of others that is beyond my ability to maneuver or orchestrate. How simple life would be if I were an orchestra conductor and all I needed to do was wave my wand, nod here and there at the various players, and the outcome would be a perfect production. Dream on! The hang-up is this issue of free will that God gave me. It's the same free will he gave to everyone else.

Children on review often say rude things. Our children grow up to make decisions we don't always feel good about. Our neighbors and political leaders sometimes choose wisely, and often make choices that don't seem sensible.

I must learn to cast my worries, small and great, "upon the Lord and he shall sustain you; he will never let the righteous fall"(Psalm 55:22). It is human nature to imagine God will be there for us in the big things like cancer, unemployment, and major catastrophes. We will certainly beg for his help. But for the nagging *✱* preoccupations that immobilize us and make us fruitless for the kingdom, we struggle on alone, worrying as we go, rather than bother the great God of the universe about our little issues. All issues are big to our heavenly Father. He cares about lilies, the hairs on our heads, even little birds. If it concerns us, he cares.

We are an impatient generation. We want circumstances to change now. We want fulfillment in every area of our lives right away. We don't have time to wait in prayer. When results don't happen instantly, we begin to worry.

Perseverance and patience

The New Testament is strangely and uncomfortably mute about immediate fulfillment, instant spirituality, and quick problem resolution. Instead, we find plenty about perseverance and patience.

I'm most prone to worry when my life's script has things on the page I would not have written there. I don't believe that this is where God wants me at this moment.

I'm a big chicken. I don't want to do the hard parts of life. I worry that it may be God's will for me that I go where I don't want to go, and do what I don't want to do. I look at the saints of the past like Corrie ten Boom, Dietrich Bonhoeffer, and Jim Elliott, and I echo the words of Mother Teresa who said, "If this is how you treat your friends, no wonder you don't have many."

Yet God's ways are higher than our ways. The testimonies of ten Boom, Bonhoeffer, and Elliott speak loud and clear long after their deaths. While in prison, the Apostle Paul wrote the epistles that continue to be a compass for us today. Also while in prison, John Bunyan wrote his classic *Pilgrim's Progress*. These believers would not have chosen this script. Yet God did not abandon his beloved in the dungeon but manifested his great power through these submitted lives.

A basic descriptive word for life is struggle – either we are in a struggle or preparing for it. When the trials of life appear too long and I question whether God sees, or hears, or cares about my fears, Psalm 27:13–14 reminds me that "I am still confident of this: I will see the goodness of the Lord in the land of the living. Wait for the Lord; be strong and take heart and wait for the Lord."

Mountaintop message

A natural teacher, Jesus recognized a teachable moment when a jostling crowd gathered in Judea. Luke records these profound words of life (Luke 12:22–32):

> *Therefore I tell you, do not worry about your life, what you will eat; or about your body, what you will wear. Life is more than food, and the body more than clothes. Consider the ravens: They do not sow or reap, they have no storeroom or barn; yet God feeds them. And how much more valuable you are than birds! Who of you by worrying can add a single hour to his life? Since you cannot do this very little thing, why do you worry about the rest?*
>
> *Consider how the lilies grow. They do not labor or spin. Yet I tell you, not even Solomon in all his splendor was dressed like one of these. If that is how God clothes the grass of the field, which is here today, and tomorrow is thrown into the fire, how much more will he clothe you, O you of little faith! And do not set your heart on what you will eat or drink; do not worry about it. For the pagan world runs after all such things, and your Father knows that you need them. But seek his kingdom, and these things will be given to you as well.*
>
> *Do not be afraid, little flock, for your Father has been pleased to give you the kingdom.*

To put the issue in perspective, Jesus plucked a lily and held it up as he spoke to the crowd. Lilies were the dandelions of the day. They were not important. They grew wild. He did not choose something precious. He chose something beautiful, but common and replaceable. Gesturing to the sky, he indicated the ravens. The blackbirds and crows of our society. Useless and dirty, they were scavengers. When it says that God feeds the birds, it does not imply that we can be lazy and not work. The important thing is that God provides the food, and gives us the ability to work in order that we have food and clothing. Even the birds have to scratch around.

We are not born worriers. We learn it. We practice it. And we get really good at it. I know someone who, when he hears of an illness, asks for the symptoms because he wants to be sure he doesn't have that. That's an overactive imagination borrowing worry. We must unlearn those kinds of reactions.

Worry is

Worry is destructive. It destroys our health, and strangles our creativity. You know how you can worry something apart? "Worry" is an Anglo-Saxon word for "strangle". The root of the word "anxious" means to pull apart. Corrie ten Boom said, "Worry does not empty tomorrow of its sorrow, it empties today of its strength."

Worry blinds us. We think we are doing something good when we worry. We are proving that we love our children because we worry about them. But that is not a demonstration of love – that is a demonstration of a lack of faith and trust in God.

Worry is unreasonable. It is a false view of life. We don't view it as a negative behavior; we might even see it as a virtue. While other people are flighty, we worriers are serious. We are brighter, deeper. Concerned about others, international affairs, and world peace. We are capable of worrying where other, more shallow types, can't. About food and clothing, no, we would never worry about that. We worry about important things. We worry about things we can't change.

What about the things we *can* change? The problem with worry is that we lose proportion. That's why I believe in writing things down, and praying out loud. I don't do it that often, but one of the things about praying out loud, is that I actually hear the worry as it really is, not just in my mind. Sometimes when I share the worry with someone, as soon as I finish, I already know. Just getting it out, deals with it. I'm reminded to trust God with the things that cannot be changed.

The problem is not God's disinterest. We don't worry if God *can* answer our prayers. *Will* he answer our request is the real question. It is not a question of his power, but we sometimes worry about his willingness to do what we ask him.

Proud and arrogant, we have bad habits. The habit of worry is depressing, debilitating, and unhelpful. We cannot change our past, we cannot control the future, but we can sure ruin today. The only thing we have the power to control is the hour in which we live. Worry stunts our growth. It hinders us from trying anything.

The antidote

The antidote to worry is faith and trust.

Trust is the outworking of faith. Just as worry is fear in action, trust is faith in action. Trust is gained through practice, exercise, and deliberate concentration. When I was a little girl, I memorized a verse called "I will trust, and not be afraid." It even has a little tune I could sing for you. I was probably taught this in a tiny, one-room Sunday school for children of all ages. Some sixty years later, I still remember it. Trust is the awareness of danger and risk, coupled with a deliberate decision to actively move ahead, confidently trusting all scary and not-so-scary outcomes to the heavenly Father.

Begin with baby steps. Look for success in the short run. I wrote this book one paragraph at a time. Thinking about the whole project gave me a headache and made me break out in a chronic case of worry.

"The weapons we fight with are not the weapons of the world. On the contrary, they have divine power to demolish strongholds. We demolish arguments and every pretension that sets itself up against the knowledge of God, and we take captive every thought to make it obedient to Christ" (2 Corinthians 10:4–5). "Casting down imaginations, and every high thing that exalteth itself against the knowledge of God" is the King James version of this verse. Imaginations and pretensions are our thoughts about what might happen, the predictions a doctor might make, what statistics tell us. This scripture instructs me to consciously refuse gloomy thoughts, focusing my mind on God's promises. Nor does Paul grant any wiggle room about worrying. He tells us to take captive "every" thought. Jesus instructs, "Don't worry."

Fear and worry is a choice. I can choose to not be troubled by believing the promises of the Lord written out for me in Scripture. I choose what I believe. I remember mulling over (worrying over) the statistics I had been given regarding my kind of cancer, my age, and the lymph node involvement. I used all my math skills as I factored in the mitigating factors to the oncologist's statement; an 85 per cent probability of living five years. Who wants five years? I wanted more. And what about that 15 per cent? Am I in there somewhere?

Into my middle-of-the-night wakefulness came the promises of Scripture. I chose to rehearse those rather than statistics.

Turn worry into productivity. Look at tomorrow's page on the calendar. Could you get a jump start on the next day's burdens tonight? With a bit of creativity, there may be some simple ways to reduce worry by being better prepared for what's ahead.

I choose to worry. God does not command us in Scripture to do something he knows we are incapable of doing. "Do not be anxious about anything, but in everything, by prayer and petition, with thanksgiving, present your requests to God" (Philippians 4:6). The Lord instructs us to choose not to worry, and to choose to bring our concerns to him in prayer. We are not asked to do the impossible.

> But I trust in your unfailing love;
> my heart rejoices in your salvation.
> I will sing to the Lord,
> for he has been good to me.
>
> PSALM 13:5–6

King David's Old Testament prescription is as relevant today as it was when he wrote the Psalms. For such a time as this, he employed a three-pronged approach. He traded his worry for trusting, rejoicing, and singing. Yes, it is right to ask questions of God. "Come, let us reason together," the Lord invites. Abraham questioned and debated with God about Sodom and Gomorrah's fate in Genesis.

Job questioned God's actions and motives. Job never did get an answer to the great big *why*. God ignored the question and gave the response that he knew Job really needed. God revealed himself slowly to Job, helping him see who he was dealing with. "I know that my Redeemer lives, and that in the end he will stand upon the earth... yet in my flesh I shall see God" (Job 19:25–26). This was Job's big "Aha!" moment.

Go ahead, ask

Questions and discussion do not offend the Creator of the Universe. He doesn't get angry or lose patience. I believe he enjoys an academic conversation. But don't

expect him to answer as you demand. He answered
Job, but certainly not the way Job pictured it. He is a
good God, but as C. S. Lewis said, "He's not tame." In
his own darkest hours, Jesus too asked "Why?" Godly
people have always asked questions and will continue
to do so.

Often our honest questions lead us to trust, to
rejoice, and to sing, even when we don't get answers.
Andrew Murray said, "In times of questions, I say four
things: I am here by God's appointment; I am here in
his keeping; I am here under his training; I am here
for his time."

What about those fears that wake you in the
night? David's prescription for wakeful nights in the
desert of Judah was:

On my bed I remember you;
I think of you through the watches of the night.
Because you are my help,
I sing in the shadow of your wings.
My soul clings to you;
your right hand upholds me.

PSALM 63:6–8

When my world appears to be spinning out of my
control, it is still in God's control. "I know that you can
do all things; no plan of yours can be thwarted" (Job
42:2). Psalm 103:19 echoes, "The Lord established his
throne in heaven, and his kingdom rules over all."

When I don't understand the Lord's ways, that's
where trust comes in. "Oh, the depth of the riches of

the wisdom and knowledge of God! How unsearchable his judgments, and his paths beyond tracing out!" (Romans 11:33).

When I worry that God may allow harsh trials in my life, Scripture tells me, "For great is your love, higher than the heavens; your faithfulness reaches to the skies" (Psalm 108:4).

When I'm worried that life has been reduced to a rat race and the rats are winning, Scripture responds, "For the Lord is righteous, he loves justice; upright men will see his face" (Psalm 11:7).

When I'm being bullied, intimidated, and treated unfairly, Psalm 37:1 coaches, "Do not fret because of evil men or be envious of those who do wrong; for like the grass they will soon wither, like green plants they will soon die away."

The Lord's commands enable us. He gives us power through his Holy Spirit to obey his Word. "The one who calls you is faithful and he will do it" (1 Thessalonians 5:24).

To win over worry means to submit the worries to the One who carries them. Then their ability to control or influence is reduced. Look to the long perspective. At the beginning of a new year, I look back over the past one and say, "Is progress being made? Am I trusting more?" We win when vast amounts of time go by and we realize that it has been so very long since the fear even came to mind, let alone affected behavior. And we honor the One through whom it happened.

Include God in the dailyness of life. "I don't need you now. I'll let you know when I do," is the antithesis of a growing relationship with the Lord. I don't call on slight acquaintances in calamity. In a crisis, I dial a number I know by heart. When I'm accustomed to bringing my worries to the Lord, I will know the character of my Savior and call on him because he is near and I trust him.

> *Lord, help me not to dream what might happen,*
> *Not to worry about what could happen,*
> *But to accept what does happen*
> *Because you care for me.*
>
> DOROTHY MOFFITT

> *When you think about a problem over and over in your mind, that's called worry. When you think about God's Word over and over in your mind, that's meditation. If you know how to worry, you know how to meditate!*
>
> RICK WARREN, *THE PURPOSE DRIVEN LIFE*

APPLICATION POINT

1. Regarding that issue you are worrying about, what is the worst thing that could happen?

2. Mark Twain said that the great majority of our anxieties never happen. How much time do you spend worrying over things that never occur? How much time do you waste worrying over things that you can't control anyway?

STEPPING OUT

Martin Luther is reputed to have said, "I cannot stop the birds from flying over my head, but I can keep them from making a nest in my hair." We can keep worries from lodging in our thoughts. Learn to trust God for the big issues by trusting him with the small stuff. Practice constant communication by making your worries a conversation with the Lord.

CHAPTER 5

THE DARK NIGHT OF THE
BODY AND SOUL

The Lord will guide you always;
he will satisfy your needs in a sun-scorched land
and will strengthen your frame.
You will be like a well-watered garden,
like a spring whose waters never fail.

ISAIAH **58:11**

Fear not, I am with thee, Oh be not dismayed.
For I am thy God and will still give thee aid.
I'll strengthen thee, help thee, and cause thee to stand
Upheld by my gracious, omnipotent hand.
When through fiery trials thy pathway shall lie
My grace, all sufficient, shall be thy supply.
The flame shall not hurt thee, I only design
Thy dross to consume and thy gold to refine.
The soul that on Jesus hath leaned for repose
I will not, I will not desert to his foes.
That soul, though all hell should endeavor to shake

87

I'll never, no never, no never forsake.

JOHN RIPPON, "HOW FIRM A FOUNDATION,"

FROM A 1787 HYMNAL

"I want to live."

I penned those words in my journal one day in June. Summer was in the air. I was a young mother with four active boys and a husband dedicated to ministry. The diagnosis was breast cancer. "I cry to my Father like a small child and tell him I'm afraid."

A friend said, "I've experienced times when I hide deep under the covers of my bed and whisper, 'Abba! Owie, it hurts!' I cry myself to sleep in the shelter of his comforting arms. I always feel better after."

Cancer and chronic illness wield fear as a weapon against our already tenuous health. We even describe these situations in ways that eliminate much sense of hope. The words that easily tumble from our mouths reflect our faith. Or lack of it.

I refuse to say:

- I'm battling cancer.

- I'm fighting cancer.

- I'm struggling against cancer.

- I had a life-threatening illness.

I will say:

- A person is living with cancer.

- I had a life-altering illness.

• We have hope for comfort and ease.

• As Christians, we have the promise of a permanent address in heaven.

God is not surprised when a situation appears humanly impossible. Hopeless. We can accept our emotions and stay positive because Jesus lived here, too. When circumstances look dismal at best and we're tempted to kiss ourselves goodbye, Scripture reminds us that God has the final word.

Cancer and its cousin, chronic illness, bring along an unwanted pest called depression. Depression is a deep, dark pit. It is anger turned inward. It can become severe. Human beings can be neurotic, even Christians. Many of us have experienced dark periods. I have wrestled with unexplained gloom. As the Lord moved me out of those periods, he allowed me to hurt with the hurts of my friends, to almost physically feel when someone is hurting.

Too often we have to walk a road we did not choose. Jesus experienced a dark night of the soul. Being fully God and fully man, Jesus knew what agonies awaited as he put one foot in front of the other. As he made his way to Jerusalem, he faced death. A torturous death.

Christ's dark night of the soul

After the Passover, as was his custom, Jesus went to the Mount of Olives. Though people generally prayed standing up, Jesus knelt in an olive grove called

Gethsemane and poured out his fears. "Father, if you are willing, take this cup from me; yet not my will, but yours, be done" (Luke 22:42).

The cup was a symbol of suffering and divine anger. In his humanness, it was natural for Christ to shrink from the horror of the cross. Which of us wouldn't? None of us would want to experience that cruel death. Knowing he would bear the weight of divine anger on sin and be forsaken by God multiplied his anguish. "And being in anguish, he prayed more earnestly, and his sweat was like drops of blood falling down to the ground" (Luke 22:44).

Jesus experienced deep betrayal and failure. After pouring three years of work and mentoring into his hand-picked followers, he was forsaken by those closest to him in his greatest hour of need.

"Then he said to them, 'My soul is overwhelmed with sorrow to the point of death. Stay here and keep watch with me'" (Matthew 26:38). During that pivotal night in history, Jesus could have watched events unfold. Watched his impending fate. From his prayer vigil on the Mount of Olives, he had a clear view across the Kidron Valley to the Antonias. As darkness fell, torches would have lit the main military establishment in Jerusalem, located to the north of the Temple. Before long, the bobbing torches of a crowd, sent from the chief priests and teachers of the law, could be seen making their way from the city, snaking down the winding trail through the Kidron Valley. It is nearly a thirty-minute walk from the city to the bottom of the valley, and nearly the same time to climb the far side to Gethsemane. For the better part of an hour, Christ could have observed the angry mob coming for him.

But after his own dark night of the soul in the garden, Jesus found his friends sleeping. We hear the pain of betrayal in his voice when he says to Peter, James, and John, "What! Could you not watch with Me one hour?" (Matthew 26:40, NKJV).

Moments later, Judas, one of Jesus' inner circle, arrived with a mob brandishing swords and clubs. "Then all the disciples forsook Him and fled" (Matthew 26:56, NKJV).

Earlier, Jesus had predicted that Peter would deny he knew Jesus three times before morning. The soldiers roughly escorted Jesus from the Mount of Olives, back across the valley and up uneven stone steps to the Chief Priest's home in Jerusalem. Peter followed at a distance. In Caiaphas' intimate courtyard, Peter sat among the servants who kindled a fire for warmth. Three times someone accused Peter of being a follower of the man on trial. Three times, each time more fervently, Peter denied knowing the man, denied knowing his friend and teacher, Jesus. "Immediately, while he was still speaking, the rooster crowed. And the Lord turned and looked at Peter" (Luke 22:61, NKJV). "So Peter went out and wept bitterly."

We serve a Lord and Savior who understands on a personal level what we experience when we are rejected, denied, betrayed, and abandoned. When we find ourselves deep in a dark night of the soul.

Fellow travelers on the journey

Others in the Bible also found themselves depressed and discouraged. Drowning in hopelessness, they experienced a dark night of the soul. After losing his children and possessions, Job was confused and depressed for forty chapters.

For preaching Christ, Paul and Barnabas were beaten and jailed. Scripture says at midnight they began to sing. Prior to that late hour, I have no doubt they were experiencing deep discouragement.

David penned his impressions of his dark night of the soul in Psalm 88, which we may entitle 'A Prayer of Despondency':

> *For my soul is full of trouble,*
> *and my life draws near the grave.*
> *I am counted among those who go down to the pit;*
> *I am like a man without strength.*
> *I am set apart with the dead,*
> *like the slain who lie in the grave,*
> *whom you remember no more,*
> *who are cut off from your care.*
> *You have put me in the lowest pit,*
> *in darkest depths.*

PSALM 88:3–6

Fear paralyzes us and hinders us from taking responsibility. Writing to his young protégé, Paul seems to be dealing with a discouraged, fearful fellow. From the text comes the impression that

Timothy had begun so well and yet found himself depressed and losing confidence in Scripture. Timothy's ministry and his confidence to confront problems wavered. In 2 Timothy, Paul begins with a résumé of God's past dealings with Timothy through his mother and grandmother, Eunice and Lois. Knowing his time remaining to mentor Timothy is short, Paul then gives both practical and personal challenges to encourage his spiritual son (1 Timothy 4:14, 16; 2 Timothy 1:4, 6, 13). Paul's theme was simple. He admonished, "Be strong."

On Sunday, April 8, 1945, Dietrich Bonhoeffer had just finished conducting a service of worship at Schoenberg, Germany, when two soldiers entered.

"Prisoner Bonhoeffer, make ready and come with us." It was the standard summons to a condemned prisoner.

To another prisoner, Bonhoeffer confided, "This is the end – but for me, the beginning – of life." Deep in his own dark night of the soul, Bonhoeffer wrote this in his prison cell:

Who am I? They often tell me I would step from my cell's confinement calmly, cheerfully, firmly, like a squire from his country-house. Who am I? They often tell me I would talk to my warden freely and friendly and clearly, as though it were mine to command.

Who am I? They also tell me I would bear the days of misfortune equably, smilingly, proudly, like one accustomed to win. Am I then really

*all that which other men tell of, or am I only
what I know of myself, restless and longing
and sick, like a bird in a cage, struggling for
breath, as though hands were compressing my
throat, yearning for colors, for flowers, for the
voices of birds, thirsting for words of kindness,
for neighborliness, trembling with anger at
despotisms and petty humiliation, tossing
in expectation of great events, powerlessly
trembling for friends at an infinite distance,
weary and empty at praying, at thinking, at
making, faint and ready to say farewell to it all.*

*Who am I? This or the other? Am I one
person today, and tomorrow another? Am I both
at once? A hypocrite before others, and before
myself a contemptibly woebegone weakling?
Or is something within me still like a beaten
army, fleeing in disorder from victory already
achieved?*

*Who am I? They mock me, these lonely
questions of mine. Whoever I am, Thou knowest,
O God, I am thine.*

He was hanged the next day. That morning, he was observed by the prison doctor, who said: "Through the half-open door I saw Pastor Bonhoeffer still in his prison clothes, kneeling in fervent prayer to the Lord his God. The devotion and evident conviction of being heard that I saw in the prayer of this intensely captivating man moved me to the depths." Having settled who he was in Christ, Bonhoeffer was led from his cell and ordered to strip. Naked under the scaffold, Bonhoeffer knelt for one last time to pray. Five minutes later, he was dead.

Becoming stronger

One friend who has experienced a hard life too frequently found herself deep in the pit of depression. "Is there a phone in the pit?" she once asked. Indeed, there is a direct line to God.

Life is a struggle. "Consider it pure joy, my brothers, whenever you face trials of many kinds, because you know that the testing of your faith develops perseverance. Perseverance must finish its work so that you may be mature and complete, not lacking anything" (James 1:2–4). The struggle makes us stronger, though I wish there were an easier way.

Having an understanding of what the Bible says about suffering provides a well to draw upon during the crisis. Obvious conclusions include:

- Tough times come to all.

- There are several possible reasons why I am suffering.

- It may be clear why I'm suffering, or it may never make sense.

- My response is mine to display.

A neurologist friend tells me that I wouldn't want to know the percentage of the illnesses that affect us physically which all trace back to worry, stress, and a lack of trust in God.

According to an ancient legend, a man driving one day to Constantinople was stopped by an old woman who asked him for a ride. He agreed and, as they drove along, he looked at her and became frightened.

He asked, "Who are you?"

The old woman replied, "I am Cholera."

Immediately the peasant ordered the old woman to get down and walk; but she persuaded him to take her along, promising that she would not kill more than five people in Constantinople. As pledge of her promise, she handed him a dagger, the only weapon that could kill her. "I shall meet you in two days," she said. "If I break my promise, you may stab me."

In Constantinople 120 people died of cholera. Meeting the old woman, the enraged man who had driven her into the city raised the dagger to kill her.

"I have kept my agreement," she protested. "I killed only five. Fear killed the others."

The legend is a parable of life. Where disease kills its thousands, fear kills its tens of thousands. The great miseries of mankind come from the dread of catastrophe, rather than from the presence of real, rather than imagined, danger. Fear betrays man's spirit, breaks down his defense, disarms him in the battle, unfits him for the work of life, and adds terror to the death-bed.

King Saul was haunted by fear. He was initially afraid to be crowned king, and then feared he wouldn't keep his kingdom. Saul feared David's success and spent years expending troops, finances, and peace of mind chasing David throughout the Judean wilderness. His fear distracted him from being a strong leader and fractured his relationship with his children.

God is able

In a gift shop in Buenos Aires, I found a small clay image of a hand with a tiny bird resting in the palm. These figures are made by the Toba Indians in northern Argentina. When I saw the upturned hand with the delicate little bird, I immediately thought of the scriptures where God tells us how he holds us in the palm of his hand, and writes our name on his hand. "Can a mother forget the baby at her breast and have no compassion on the child she has borne? Though she may forget, I will not forget you! See, I have engraved you on the palms of my hands" (Isaiah 49:15–16).

I asked the woman attending the shop if she knew what the hand and the little bird signified. When she replied that she didn't, I quoted the promise of Jesus, "I give them eternal life, and they shall never perish; no one can snatch them out of my hand" (John 10:28). Her eyes lit up at the memory of the verse she used to know but had forgotten. I invited her to the events we were involved in where she could encounter the One who holds us securely, and personally.

I purchased the hand cradling the bird because the bird is me. As a reminder, this figure is a tangible tool to tackle terrors.

On my desk is a plaque with the words, "He is Able." The phrase appears several times in the New Testament. The words remind me that whatever my need of the moment, Jesus is sufficient. He dwells within me. He calms my fears. He does not always miraculously lift me out of my trials. The greater miracle is that he often walks with me through my challenges.

Sometimes I pretend that the fear of the day is a big rock. I place it in a large, heavy plastic bag and lay it at Jesus' feet. Then I walk away and leave it with him. Our Lord does not help us carry the load. He takes complete responsibility. We cause our own frustration when we do not totally trust Jesus. Too often I believe I can handle it alone, maybe with a little support or a lot of help from the Lord, but rarely will I cast it *all* on him. We value self-sufficiency. In the far west of America, we pride ourselves on our independent, pioneer spirit.

As 'fraidy cats, we pussy-foot around our private and personal fears. Some are for publication, and some are private. In accountability situations, do we tell the truth, the whole truth, or just enough to stay in the game? It may not matter if the real, true issues have been left where they belong – with Jesus.

I had a watch that needed repair. I took it to the repairman but until I released it out of my own hands and put it in his capable ones, the repairman could not do the necessary work. In the same way, Jesus knows that from time to time we tiptoe up and drag our care of the moment back into our own hands to rehash it and worry over it some more. The world's peace is fragile, easily set off balance, is under the dominion of circumstances, moods, pressures, temperature, seasons, world conditions, the economy, our companions, and just plain noise. Eventually we remember where our fear belongs and return it to the proper place – with the only One who can bring peace, and ultimately resolution.

Rooted in God's Word

Dealing with fear is a habit to be learned and a command to be obeyed. When I was dealing with cancer, I wrote things down – the promises of God that were tangible. I memorized verses to help me with my fears:

> • I am a child of God, and he holds me in his hand (John 10:28).

> • "The Lord is my light and my salvation – whom shall I fear? The Lord is the stronghold of my life – of whom shall I be afraid?" (Psalm 27:1).

> • "The eternal God is our refuge, and underneath are the everlasting arms" (Deuteronomy 33:27).

> • "Keep me as the apple of your eye; hide me in the shadow of your wings" (Psalm 17:8).

At times after the initial diagnosis I wondered wildly whether it was all a mistake. I felt just fine. One day a doctor said suspicious things about a tiny little lump.

Over the next week other furrowed brows looked at X-rays and specimens and said, "It's malignant." They laid plans of attack and I listened in shock, with a friend at my side who took notes and helped me ask questions.

When my imagination ran beyond reality, I would rein it back in with "Sufficient unto the day is the evil thereof" (Matthew 6:34, KJV). When mind-wasting, distracting thoughts went around in my mind like a hamster on a wheel, I slowly learned to direct my attention to the promises in Scripture regarding peace, strength, and patience. Verses I had previously known only in theory I now understood experientially. Time is limited, so why would I choose to continue to waste precious moments dwelling on negativity that fed my disease and harmed my mind?

"For as he thinks in his heart, so is he" (Proverbs 23:7). When my self-talk is contrary to the promises of God's Word, guess who is wrong? "Whatever is true, whatever is noble, whatever is right, whatever is pure, whatever is lovely, whatever is admirable – if anything is excellent or praiseworthy – think on such things," instructs Philippians 4:8. I choose to believe and plant my roots deep into the fertile soil of God's Word.

Facing my mortality put my pettiness with others and life in general in perspective. After his son died on a youth trip, a pastor said he no longer engaged in arguments about the color of his church's carpet or walls. It was all so much trivia. It didn't matter any more. Like that pastor, I learned instead to intercede for restoration for those who were wrong. The state of their soul became vitally more important than me being right.

Turning my concerns and fears into constant communion with my heavenly Father melted the gloom and I began to actually feel his love, care, and strength. I was entering exciting new territory.

I have often heard people say, "Don't think becoming a follower of Christ will make your life easier. It won't." I cannot imagine what life would be like without the stabilizing promises of Christ. While I went through my own bone scan, I prayed for a neighbor. How, I wondered, does someone face fear, pain, disease, and death without Christ? "I have set the Lord always before me. Because he is at my right hand, I will not be shaken. Therefore my heart is glad and my tongue rejoices; my body also will rest secure" (Psalm 16:8–9).

When my emotions and thoughts were as tumultuous as the storm on the Sea of Galilee, I would focus on the images that Scripture gives to describe the Lord. He is my rock, he hides me in the palm of his hand. The discipline of taking every thought captive was most necessary when I least felt capable of exerting the effort to do it. Peace returned when I returned to the promises. When my heart echoed David's cries in Psalm 62:3, "How long will you assault a man?", I countered with "My soul finds rest in God alone; my salvation comes from him. He alone is my rock and my salvation; he is my fortress, I will never be shaken" (Psalm 62:1–2). "May your God, whom you serve continually, rescue you" (Daniel 6:16).

A week after I wrote those first words in my journal, I established a morning routine:

1. Waking, my first conscious thought was a fear-riddled "It can't be!" Panic coursed though my veins like ice-water through a straw.

2. I acknowledged the fact that I did, indeed, have life-threatening cancer. Ouch!

3. I began that day's conversation with my Father by complaining honestly. Then I turned to the Scriptures for reassurance of his tangible promises. Breathing deeply and resting on the Lord, I accepted where I was. Then I set about adopting a proper attitude for the day, believing that I was healthy today, and that God cared for me. I would not consider future possibilities.

4. I determined to pray for, and help, others.

Believe me, it was work and discipline to begin my day like this. It would have been a far easier and less productive use of my time to free-fall into the very tempting pools of despair, whining, and complaining.

It was worth the effort. It was exciting to learn some of God's secrets. "Not everything that happens to you is good," a friend told me. "But God can bring good out of everything and make us more like Jesus."

And we know that in all things God works for the good of those who love him, who have been called according to his purpose. For those God

*foreknew he also predestined to be conformed to
the likeness of his Son.*

ROMANS 8:28–29

The University of Adversity

My journal bears testimony that I suffered many
dreadful days. There was a constant rehashing of
medical facts and probabilities between the doctors.
The percentage of lymph-node involvement, my age,
possible therapies and their predicted outcomes, and
my overall medical condition all added up to a giant
question mark.

"His purposes shall be accomplished," I wrote
on a dark day. "We are to rejoice in his workings and
accept results as from his sovereign hand. Never have
we personally paid such a high price to be obedient
but never have I had such deep peace. Therefore the
battle is not ours, but God's. Jesus learned obedience
by the things he suffered. I repent of the occasions
when I was not willing to pay any price to see the
Gospel proclaimed."

On days when I was emotionally weak and the
physical pain felt ominous, I was too tired to fight
attitudes of fear, morbid thoughts, and self-pity.
"Though I walk in the midst of trouble, you preserve
my life; you stretch out your hand against the anger
of my foes, with your right hand you save me. The
Lord will fulfill his purpose for me; your love, O Lord,
endures forever – do not abandon the works of your
hands" (Psalm 138:7–8).

With an unstable hand, I wrote affirmations:

1. I will feel well and strong.

2. The chemotherapy will be effective and have minimal side-effects.

3. Life will return to normal.

4. I will enjoy the new things I have learned and experienced about God, his love, his care, and his Word.

5. I will share my faith with others.

"The Lord is close to the brokenhearted and saves those who are crushed in spirit," promises Psalm 34:18. After serving the Lord for decades, from a bed of pain, missionary to India Amy Carmichael said, "If God remembers our hairs, will he not also number our tears?"

Indeed, he will. "He will wipe away every tear from their eyes. There will be no more death or mourning or crying or pain, for the old order of things has passed away" (Revelation 21:4).

Three years later, when dawn began to break over my dark night of the soul, I clutched at those lessons God had taught me in that deep pit. "Dear Lord," I wrote in my journal, "Don't let me slip back into ways I thought I had left behind. I've paid a high price to learn a few things. It's so easy to relax and think the battle is over when it is only a skirmish. I can't live at high tension either. Keep me alert, but relaxed and confident. You are in control. I shall not become complacent. I shall cherish my husband and children and show them I do. I shall not put off demonstrating love. I shall tell them how much they mean to me."

The greatest lesson I learned is that God is indeed worthy of trust.

It has been three decades since my cancer experience but certain encounters bring back memories and a sense of wonderment at God's choice to leave me here. God's answers are beyond us. They are inscrutable.

> *I would say to my soul, O my soul this is not the place of despair; this is not the time to despair in. As long as mine eyes can find a promise in the Bible, as long as there is a moment left me of breath or life in this world, so long will I wait or look for mercy, so long will I fight against unbelief and despair.*
>
> JOHN BUNYAN

APPLICATION POINT

1. What would I be like without my pet fear?

2. There are familiar steps to falling into the pit of deep despair. What *different* path can I choose to take?

STEPPING OUT

Here are some practical, tangible helps for the "square-minded" fearful soul. I used them myself, and I hope they will be beneficial to you:

1. Find a symbolic figurine and place it where it will continually remind you of God's promises. A palms-up hand cradling a tiny bird, sculpted in clay by the Toba Indians of Argentina, reminds me that I'm safe in God's capable hands.

2. Place key Scripture verses where you will see them. One of my friends uses God's Word as the décor for her home. "He is Able," written in calligraphy and resting on my desk, reminds me to turn over my worry of the day to my competent Lord. Speaking aloud, "He is able to… (heal my body, provide the finances, change a hard heart…)," calms my fears.

3. Act out the verse, "Cast all your anxiety on him because he cares for you" (1 Peter 5:7). I imagine my fear or pattern of fear is a huge boulder that I place in the bottom of a large garbage bag. What does the verse tell you and me to do with that sack?

4. On a set of three-by-five index cards, I created for myself a "Prescription for Peace." I looked up the words "peace" and "courage" in a concordance. Choosing encouraging Bible

verses, I wrote them on the cards and carried them with me. <u>Make your own courage cards</u>.

CHAPTER 6

THE FEAR TO END ALL FEARS

Since the children have flesh and blood, he too
shared in their humanity so that by his death he
might destroy him who holds the power of death
– that is, the devil – and free those who all their
lives were held in slavery by their fear of death.

HEBREWS 2:14–15

All the days ordained for me
were written in your book
before one of them came to be.

PSALM 139:16

You ain't gonna get out of here alive.

DR PHIL

Once we are followers of Christ, where we are going
is not the issue – that's already been determined. The
issue is who we are becoming.

There are all kinds of stories about the foolishness

of fear. One that used to go around was about a middle-aged widow whose grown son laid on the couch all day and refused to do anything.

"Move him out," her counselor advised.

"I couldn't do that," she said.

"Why not? What would be the worst that could happen?"

"He wouldn't get a job, he'd be on the streets, he'd be hungry, and he would get sick."

"What's the worst that could happen?" the counselor asked again.

"He could die," she lamented.

That's the bottom line, isn't it? If we follow our fears, most of them end on that note. "Everybody's afraid to live," said Jimmy Stewart in the film, *You Can't Take it With You*, noting that most people are motivated by fear, afraid to eat, afraid to drink, afraid of their job, their future, their health. Scared to save money and scared to spend it. The media commercialize on fear, scare you to death so they can sell you what you don't need.

If the worst that could happen is that we could die, what's so bad about that? We're believers in the Lord Jesus Christ and eternal life, after all. Yet, the fear of death is the granddaddy of them all. It's the behind-the-scenes threat that pushes, drives, and motivates most of our besetting fears. Death is the ultimate loss of control.

Death is in the background of every fear. Unfortunately it is fairly well grounded in reality. The bad news bulletin is, short of Christ's promised return, we will all die. Someone said you can't run from the inevitable, you'll just die tired. The death toll in previous generations is 100 per cent (with the exception of Enoch and Elijah). As the saying goes, nothing is sure but death and taxes. It is inevitable. Man is "destined to die once, and after that to face judgment" (Hebrews 9:27).

On a trip to England, I toured Westminster Abbey with a dear friend. Despite their royalty, positions, and wealth, kings and queens are entombed in that historic and breathtaking cathedral. My friend penned her thoughts:

> *The rooms*
> *of tombs*
> *where still, cold marble figures lie.*
> *Poor, common mortals*
> *in the end.*
> *For even*
> *kings and queens*
> *must*
> *die.*

KATHLEEN LEWIS

There are plenty of other inevitabilities like getting older, experiencing pain and disappointment. So why are we so afraid of something that is going to happen no matter what? Why are we scared to death of death? The greater tragedy, the heartbreaking crisis is that anyone dies without knowing the Good News of Jesus Christ.

No matter how we play with the language – using euphemisms such as "died," "passed," "went to be with the Lord," "graduated to glory" – the subject is not high on our comfort level. Just read the sympathy cards for avoidance terminology.

Created for immortality

In our early years of missionary work in Latin America, Luis and I were stationed in Cali, Colombia. Our third son, Andrew, was born there. When Luis received invitations to preach the Good News in the neighboring countries, I didn't go because the three little boys were too young, and the conditions were too primitive.

In about 1967, Luis went for several weeks to minister among the indigenous people of Peru. In some places, the altitude is over 15,000 feet. Ironically, this is an area where people work far underground in copper mines.

When Luis returned to his little family, he recounted the extreme cold which kept them in sleeping bags all day until it was time for the meetings, and then chased them right back under covers again. The ministers were cared for by gracious couples who were thankful that he and a musician had come.

One morning Luis asked, "Has anyone ever come from Lima, or another country to preach for you before?"

"Oh, yes, brother. A pastor came last year but upon leaving, *el dejo de existir.*" How's your high school Spanish? The pastor, they ever so diplomatically explained, had "ceased to exist." What a gentle euphemism! No one wanted to discourage this year's evangelist.

Perhaps because we were created in the Garden of Eden for immortality, we are profoundly uncomfortable with death, especially our own. Any parent who experiences the death of a child faces our own powerlessness over this dark specter. Tony Woodlief writes:

> *My daughter taught me the deepest humility, at least for a man, which is knowing I can't always protect what I love. Her tumor was a murderous intruder, but I couldn't kill it. I could only watch and pray and grieve. She was the one who reminded us, as we held her and wept after learning there would be no cure, that "Daddy, God says don't worry about tomorrow."*

When we follow all our worst worries to their end – we worry about our kids and loved ones because they may fail, and ultimately they might die. We worry that we may fail and ultimately we might die.

The fear of death is the incentive for most of the precautions that we take. It is why we notice every ache or pain. When someone does not have a desire to live, that is abnormal and we take it very seriously. The majority of us will be dragged out of here kicking and screaming. Our zest for life is part of the way God has hard-wired us. Life is precious to the Creator and he built that instinctual value into us. God made us to cling to and "love life and see good days" (1 Peter 3:10).

Our worst fear is, "I could die." And, that is the point! We will. And all our fears will end. We fight God's greatest gift to us. We love life and hang on, and on, and on. I had an elderly friend and one day I said to her, "By now, Nana, you must be anxious to go to heaven."

"Not right now," she replied. "Maybe later."

Nana was 93 at that time. We have to be, as the hymn says, "weaned from earth." Someone said that when we get to heaven we will have two thoughts. First, we will be awestruck at the magnificence. Second, we will wonder why God had to drag us kicking and screaming to get there. Why didn't we come running?

Security in Christ

The end of the journey is that we die. And then we go to heaven – if we are a child of God. "If you confess with your mouth, 'Jesus is Lord,' and believe in your heart that God raised him from the dead, you will be saved" (Romans 10:9). "Yet to all who received him, to those who believed in his name, he gave the right to be become children of God" (John 1:12). So what's to be afraid of?

For most of us, the way we leave this world will be through death. Why is that such a bother? It's scary because we've not done it before, nor do we have any reliable witness, outside of Scripture, to tell us what it is like. We always fear the unknown. The only One who has tasted death is the One who will take us through it. "But we see Jesus, who was made a little lower than the angels, now crowned with glory and honor because he suffered death, so that by the grace of God he might taste death for everyone" (Hebrews 2:9). He will go with us even in death.

A personal parenthesis: I don't believe a word of anyone who says they have been dead and have come back to tell us about it. Dead is dead. When the hamster died, my children wanted me to do something about it. Fix it. When the goldfish died, putting it back in the water only made it float on its back.

It is appointed unto man, the Scripture says, to die *once*. And after that is judgment. Though it is an interesting subject, no one has ever come back to tell us what is it like. Psalm 23 has a tremendous message. "Though I walk through the valley of the shadow of death, I will fear no evil," the Psalmist wrote. The shadow of death is merely that – the shadow. Not the real thing for Christians. The fear we have because we have not done it before is compensated by the promise that we will not do it alone. The only one who tasted death for each one of us will take us through the experience.

Those who call Jesus Christ their Lord have eternal life. God places eternal value on each of us. "So don't be afraid; you are worth more than any sparrow" (Matthew 10:31).

Do we fear that God will reject us? The Psalmist expressed these questions we all ask:

Why, O Lord, do you stand far off?
Why do you hide yourself in times of trouble?

How long, O Lord?
Will you forget me forever?
How long will you hide your face from me?
How long must I wrestle with my thoughts
and every day have sorrow in my heart?
How long will my enemy triumph over me?

Will the Lord reject forever?
Will he never show his favor again?
Has his unfailing love vanished forever?
Has his promise failed for all time?
Has God forgotten to be merciful?
Has he in anger withheld his compassion?

PSALMS 10:1; 13:1–2; 77:7–9

The Scriptures give us hope, not only for the present, but also for eternity. "I will never leave you; never will I forsake you" (Hebrews 13:5), promises our Lord. "We are confident, I say, and will prefer to be away from the body and at home with the Lord" (2 Corinthians 5:8). If the ultimate fear – death – becomes a reality, God has promised me heaven. I am sure of that. This is not a pat answer to avoid an uncomfortable theme. It is the truth that gives answers, the definitive reality in a world that sometimes makes no sense. "Where can I go from your Spirit? Where can I flee from your presence?" (Psalm 139:7).

Certainly we are not afraid of spending all of

eternity with our beloved Lord and Savior, Jesus Christ. "No eye has seen, no ear has heard, no mind has conceived what God has prepared for those who love him" (1 Corinthians 2:9).

We are scared to leave this life that is familiar to us. We aren't ready to stop exploring the many opportunities of this world, and we don't want to be separated even temporarily from loved ones. And in moments of honesty, we admit we struggle to trust God's Word regarding heaven and eternity. We can't imagine a place where no more tears are shed. We can't imagine being happy away from all that we love and hold dear here on dear old earth.

Strange but true, each one of us spends hours fighting shadows. Shadows of doubt, shadows of fear, shadows of uncertainty, and even the shadow of death. Yet a shadow has no substance and cannot harm. One writer said, "Where there is shadow, there must be light." Switchfoot wrote, "The shadow proves the sunshine (Sonshine)."

Statistics reveal that every day some 160,000 people die. For the Christ follower, statistics are not our destiny. You can't have heaven without death. But the promise of heaven takes some of the sting out of death's inevitability. The assurance of eternal life with our Lord and Savior, of having a permanent place where we belong, is priceless assurance.

"Do not let your hearts be troubled. Trust in God; trust also in me. In my Father's house are many rooms; if it were not so, I would have told

you. I am going there to prepare a place for you. And if I go and prepare a place for you, I will come back and take you to be with me that you also may be where I am. You know the way to the place where I am going."

Thomas said to him, "Lord, we don't know where you are going, so how can we know the way?"

Jesus answered, "I am the way, the truth, and the life. No one comes to the Father except through me."

JOHN 14:1–6

In an uncertain world full of fear and anxiety, what do we know for sure and hang on to? The "fear not" of Scripture simply means that I take God at his word and <u>leave the unknowable</u> with him. <u>It is an awesome thought that Scripture says</u> before I was born, the number of my days was known to God. But not to me! Fear can either control and distract us with what might happen, or totally dictate our lifestyle.

The deep fears that revolve around health, accidents, and disasters have as their ultimate end, "Well, I could die!" Yes, you could. And, we all will. We just don't know when. When we live tied up in knots by a morbid fear of death, life loses its joy and certainly the exciting life of faith designed by our God is out of our reach. Jesus came to free us from the fear of death. When we get even a slight mental handle on this issue, all other fears recede in intensity.

Freedom from death

The work of Jesus on the cross deals with the fear of death. When he said, "It is finished" (John 19:30), he meant that the stranglehold of sin and death was conquered, and the means of conquering fear was available. We have the capacity to live in freedom from fear.

We can know our destiny, and have absolute assurance of our heavenly home. Does it come in one "Aha!" moment? Maybe. But it is usually that plus a concerted, determined practice of bringing the fear into the light of God, calling it by name, and renouncing it on the basis of whose you are and who he is. When faith grows, fear dies.

God said to Abram, "Do not be afraid, Abram. I am your shield, your very great reward"(Genesis 15:1). God said, "I Am" protection and provision. Today we ask the same question. Will I be safe? Will I be fed?

The Lord assures us that we are more valuable than little creatures or the flowers of the field. Even our hairs are numbered. Christ lived among us and knows us uniquely. He kept reminding us to trust (John 14:6). When the crowds had disappeared and the rumblings from the religious leaders were growing louder, the disciples grew anxious. Judas had already begun his evil betrayal. Real danger lurked just around the corner for these friends of Jesus. Of course they were troubled – their lives were in danger. He told them, "Don't be troubled. You trust God, now trust in me."

But nothing goes to waste in God's perfect

economy. The Lord uses our own experience with fear to move us out of ourselves and allow us to relate to the fears of our friends. "Praise be to the God and Father of our Lord Jesus Christ, the Father of compassion and the God of all comfort, who comforts us in all our troubles, so that we can comfort those in any trouble with the comfort we ourselves have received from God. For just as the sufferings of Christ flow over into our lives, so also through Christ our comfort overflows" (2 Corinthians 1:3–5).

The Lord knows how we feel because he entered every area we experience. Every area of life. He tasted death for every man (Hebrews 2:9). He conquered death. Death no longer has a sting for the believer in Christ Jesus.

George Thomas, Lord Tonypandy, a long-time Speaker of the House of Commons, and a very dear friend of ours, had an extended history of poor health, including cancer. As a single man, he also dealt with loneliness. In his lilting Welsh accent he said, "What we believe decides how we behave in sickness and in health. No need to be afraid as you are not alone. Whatever happens, you will be the victor. To leave this world with Jesus is a wonderful thing."

So the answer to our ultimate fear is that someday we will be with the Lord Jesus. He is preparing a place for us. He's also interceding for us, and by his Spirit, he dwells within his children. Either way we win.

Facing the end of my own life was impetus for me to commit to living the life I have even better. In my journal I wrote:

Things I shall never go back to:
1. *Bitterness. About ministry, jealousy over the work others have been called to do.*
2. *Materialism. Not to the degree that I felt it before.*
3. *Critical spirit.*
4. *I will not be so closed-mouth about my faith in God.*
5. *Hardness toward suffering – my own and the suffering of others.*
6. *Less tolerance for trash – poor choices in media and literature.*

New things I'm embracing:
1. *Love of, and dependence on, the Word.*
2. *A deep sense of my Father's care for me.*
3. *A clear sense of safety. I will be well, not for my comfort but to be totally his.*

A short life is not an incomplete life.

J. VERNON MCGEE

The Lord is a refuge for the oppressed,
a stronghold in times of trouble.
Those who know your name will trust in you,
for you, Lord, have never forsaken those who seek you.

PSALM 9:9–10

It seems as if the powers of darkness have been allowed a lot of rope, but the end of the rope is in the hands of an omnipotent God.

J. OSWALD SANDERS

APPLICATION POINT

1. What things could you do if you weren't afraid of death?

2. How would you live if you weren't afraid?

STEPPING OUT

Focus your thoughts on the positive. When I was sick, I bought new furniture, prayed for Luis's upcoming Australia crusade, sent my oldest boys to college, dug into the Beatitudes in a Bible study, and planned family trips. Embrace your future. Make plans.

CHAPTER 7

BODY, SOUL, AND SPIRIT

*God knows where we are. Sometimes we forget
this. Sometimes we feel that God has even
forgotten us. He hasn't. God knows exactly
where we are. So, when you are afflicted with
those forsaken feelings, when you are on the
verge of throwing a pity party, thanks to those
despairing thoughts, go back to the Word of
God. God says, "I know where you are."*

CHARLES SWINDOLL

*For the word of God is living and active.
Sharper than any double-edged sword, it
penetrates even to dividing soul and spirit, joints
and marrow; it judges the thoughts and attitudes
of the heart.*

HEBREWS 4:12

During those three years when I underwent surgery
and chemotherapy, I often wondered why I talked out
of both sides of my mouth at the same time.

Someone would ask, "How are you doing?"

"Quite well," I would answer. "The Lord is near and I'm trusting him with my future."

Indeed, that was true. In between I sometimes woke to abject terror. Moments later, self-pity stole over my thoughts, making me wonder, "Will I ever again...?" How could two polarized responses come from the same person?

On lonely days I complained that no one came to visit, no one cared. I was resentful of the time that fighting the disease robbed from my days, my family, and my life. I resented that I didn't understand this awful illness that had invaded my body without my consent. I felt out of control and violated.

For my body and soul, my medical advisors encouraged me to cry. To release the pent-up emotions from my system. When cancer challenged my mortality, my body impacted my soul, and my spirit was energized by the Holy Spirit, who lives in me and whispered, "You are precious to me. I will never leave you nor forsake you."

What is the difference between my body, my soul, and my spirit? And how do they work in concert with one another? God is a Trinity of Father, Son, and Holy Spirit. Created in his image, man is also a trinity of body, soul, and spirit. It's very difficult to understand sometimes, but we move between the body, the soul, and the spirit. And each has different functions. As there is often an overlapping between the Father, the Son, and the Spirit, there is often overlapping between our body, soul, and spirit.

Body. I have one. It ties me to the ground. I don't always like it.

Ray Stedman's daughter jumped up on her parents' bed one morning. Dad pretended to be asleep.

His daughter pried open his eyelid. "Daddy! Are you in there, Daddy?"

Even a small child knows that the real person lives inside that sleepy body. My self-image, such as it is, is dictated by the acceptance of the body God gave me. "Do you not know that your body is a temple of the Holy Spirit, who is in you, whom you have received from God? You are not your own; you were bought at a price. Therefore honor God with your body" (1 Corinthians 6:19–20).

The soul senses fear naturally. My soul thinks, feels, and decides. Or, more technically, it is composed of mind, emotions, and will. When I listen to music and am affected emotionally, that's the soul at work. When my mind submits to whispers that go round and round, and I feel fear, that's my mind and body at work. When I decide to take action about those fearful feelings, and pick up my Bible, that's my will in the equation. When the realization of what I am dealing with brings morose thoughts, I speak from the area of my body in concert with my soul.

Soul is the part of us that makes habits, and thinks, and contains our mind, our emotions, and our will. Our spirit is where we call upon God to deliver us. We know God. "He who unites himself with the Lord is one with him in spirit" (1 Corinthians 6:17). But if the area of our soul is plagued by worry and fear, we will be affected in our body and our spirit.

Spirit. Now, this is the part of me that is more difficult to put a finger on. The body and soul seem like they have the situation pretty well under control. But, oh my, what a big percentage of the real me is yet to be discovered! My spirit is eternal, and can worship God. The part of me that lives forever is my spirit. The part of me that is capable of worshipping God, that is my spirit.

Jesus dialoged with a woman by a well in Samaria. "Yet a time is coming and has now come when the true worshipers will worship the Father in spirit and truth, for they are the kind of worshipers the Father seeks. God is spirit, and his worshipers must worship in spirit and in truth" (John 4:23–24).

When I respond to the Holy Spirit's nudging through my conscience, that's my spirit. When I suffer loss and I mourn and cry, the soul is responding but my redeemed spirit says, "All is well. Life is tough, but heaven is my home." My spirit receives the Word of God and says this is truth and life-affirming. I'm grateful for everyone who shared Scripture in any way with me during my recuperation and ever since.

From theory to reality

I did my share of grumbling, both in university and seminary, about the uselessness of big theological words and concepts. Especially the night before the paper was due. I remember thinking, "Who cares if man was created body, soul, and spirit?" The tri-part nature of man. What practical use does this information have for you and me today?

My illness took dry theology and made me deeply grateful for the information stored away for that evil day that Paul warns us about in Ephesians 6. It became the Living Word. I learned experientially in those days what had been pure mental understanding before.

In Genesis 1:26–27 God said, "Let us make man in our image, in our likeness." And he did. "So God created man in his own image, in the image of God he created him; male and female he created them" (Genesis 1:27). When the text uses the word "us" it is clearly teaching that the Trinity – Father, Son, and Holy Spirit – were involved in the creation of a human being.

As a human being, Adam was created body, soul, and spirit. At that point it was just God, Adam, and the animal world. God gave Adam the responsibility of naming those animals, maybe also thinking that Adam would figure out how he was distinct from the animal world.

He, and we, are distinct, you know. Not part of that kingdom. God and we humans can create, communicate, and evaluate. We can say some things are good and some things are not. Humans have a moral sense, a conscience. We are able to feel something resembling guilt regarding our own actions. This is part of the image of God.

When man first came from the hand of God, he was whole. Man was made in the image and likeness of God. In God's image, Adam displayed a likeness and connectedness to how his Creator did things, how the Creator saw things. Before the fall in the Garden of Eden, there was both image and likeness. But when sin entered the picture, the image and likeness of God was forever tarnished. Today, you and I still have the image of God, but the likeness is gone. Since we are redeemed by the cross of Jesus Christ, even that "likeness" will return. We shall be like him. "How great is the love the Father has lavished on us, that we should be called children of God! And that is what we are!" (1 John 3:1).

This is reflected in our attitudes. Our attitudes are wrong. We believe false messages, take them as facts and then act upon them. That's fear. We are bound to our fears by thought patterns which are deeply ingrained. We've been at it for years.

Ray Steadman, one of our great mentors, said:

> *There is an essence of humanity that is the*
> *greatness that God created within us when he*
> *made us in his image… We are not insignificant.*
> *There is something unaccountably grand*
> *about human beings, some hidden specialness*
> *that God placed inside us – something that*
> *was marred and distorted by sin but that still*
> *glimmers within us.*

The wonder of the gospel is that we have been redeemed. Body, soul, and spirit. That is the Good News. My spirit is as rescued as it's ever going to be.

It's home free. But through the rest of life, with its foibles and fears, God is bringing body and soul into conformity to his dear Son.

Learning to lean

Fanny Crosby, who lived most her life without sight, wrote about that restoration of the image of God through redemption:

> *Down in the human heart, crushed by the tempter,*
> *Feelings lie buried that grace can restore.*
> *Touched by a loving heart, wakened by kindness*
> *Chords that are broken will vibrate once more*
> *Rescue the perishing, care for the dying*
> *Jesus is merciful, Jesus will save.*

When we have fear, it goes through our body, soul, and spirit. The work of Christ in our hearts and lives begins by removing our greatest fear – the fear of death and condemnation. But it doesn't stop there. The active work of Christ continues in our lives through our body, soul, and spirit. What is theory becomes practice as I learn to cast all my care (fear) upon him, for he cares about me.

> *What have I to dread? What have I to fear?*
> *Leaning on the everlasting arms,*
> *I have blessed peace,*
> *With my Lord so near,*
> *Leaning on the everlasting arms.*

Leaning, leaning, safe and secure from all alarms,
Leaning, leaning, leaning on the everlasting arms.
ELISHA A. HOFFMAN AND ANTHONY J. SHOWALTER

Leaning. I can do that. I get tired a lot, physically, emotionally, and even spiritually. My eyes are always looking for a wall to lean on. Somehow, it takes the weight off my entire body. Sometimes I lean on my husband. I think he likes to be a leaning post. So does Jesus. His arms are capable. He has all the strength I need. Deuteronomy 33:27 says, "The eternal God is your refuge, and underneath are the everlasting arms."

This is also my airplane verse. In moments of turbulence when my soul is scared to death, I visualize the God who created the universe, the air, the airplane, the pilot and me, and he will keep us flying.

As Michelangelo saw an angel in a block of stone and set about to carve it out, so God sees the image of himself in fallen, frightened, degraded people. He sets about to bring that image back into full focus. When I discovered the reality and presence and activities of my spirit back in those fearful cancer days, I was actually becoming conscious of a part of me which had always existed. The part of me that worshipped with a pure heart and fearlessly expressed confidence in God's providential care over me, also dwelt in a body that was suffering and putting pressure on my mind, my emotions, and my ability to make reasonable, wise decisions. That's where the crying and gloomy thoughts came from.

As long as I live in a body, contending with my

mind, emotions, and ability to choose (my soul), there will always be a conflict between what is true and what I fear. The good news is that not only am I a tri-part being, as my theology professor taught me, but my spirit is indwelt by God himself. Whether I live or die, I am the Lord's beloved. When God and I face any challenge, temptation, trial, or tribulation, God wins!

> *The adventurous life is not one exempt from fear, but on the contrary, one that is lived in full knowledge of fears of all kinds, one in which we go forward in spite of our fears.*
>
> PAUL TOURNIER

APPLICATION POINT

1. What keeps you from leaning on God for your physical, emotional, and spiritual strength?

2. The old hymn encourages us to lean on the everlasting arms. Practice leaning, really, on anything strong enough to support you. What about the everlasting arms of Jesus? Are they capable?

Stepping out

Here are some Bible references which contain the idea or the phrase "He is Able." Look each one up and fill in the personal end of the sentence.

Jude 24: God is able to

_____.

2 Corinthians 9:8: God is able to

_____.

Romans 4:21: God is able to

_____.

2 Timothy 1:12: God is able to

_____.

Hebrews 7:25: God is able to

_____.

CHAPTER 8

THE HEART OF THE MATTER

The Word of the Lord is
a light to guide you,
a counselor to counsel you,
a staff to support you,
a sword to defend you,
and a physician to cure you.

THOMAS BROOKS

When my appliances need repair, I seek a repairman. When my car isn't functioning well, I take it to a specialist. When my body is ill, I go to a physician. When I'm scared to death, I want advice from a professional, the One who conquered fear and death.

I may not be the most fearful woman around, but I do have my issues. I may be carefree about some things, but I'm nearly paranoid about others. However, I do know where to go for answers.

Is the Bible relevant and able to help us deal with fear? Today we face issues of fear that were never dreamed of in the Old and New Testaments such as AIDS, computer viruses, and pollutants. The enormous quantity and availability of information necessitates that we exercise discernment. Statistics are tricky. The evening news and the internet cannot be trusted as pure, unadulterated, unbiased truth. While I must try to be well informed regarding things that involve my life and those I love, I cannot allow myself to be dragged from one theory to another. I am finite, and moderately educated, but I can still be snookered now and then by inadequate, incomplete, maybe even deceptive "facts".

Equilibrium comes from Scripture. The Lord calls us his "little flock" and tells us not to be afraid 365 times in Scripture. Once for every day of the year. The ultimate answer for worry, stress, anxiety, and fear is the Lord Jesus Christ.

The Bible is God's communication with us. How foolish to work around it. We trust the Holy Spirit who inspired the writers of the text. If I trust the inspiration of Scripture on ultimate issues of salvation, eternal life, and heaven, would I not also trust God's promise regarding his love and personal care for me? His constant, conscious presence with me every moment of my life is his decisive answer to my anxiety of the moment. Scripture calls to us to find rest and security in him.

It would be a Herculean feat to reference every Scripture that speaks of fear, courage, anxiety, and worry. What a reminder of the loving care of our Good Shepherd who knows our tendencies. The overemphasis of the Bible on this one theme comes from the heart of One who knows both the sickness (fear) and the cure (trust and faith).

When my fear, my pain becomes my central focus, Scripture brings me back to true north, which is God's eternal perspective. He speaks ultimates. "And the people were amazed because he spoke with authority" (Mark 1:22). Paul said, "Now we see but a poor reflection as in a mirror; then we shall see face to face. Now I know in part; then I shall know fully, even as I am fully known" (1 Corinthians 13:12).

In my cancer years, I came to see the Scriptures for what they are – the source of inner peace, food for my soul. Images from Scripture drive away fear. It puts fear in its place, which is far away from me. We have images in our minds that are not necessarily truth. We imagine what might happen based on a movie, a book, a news article, or other anecdotal material. When Luis told one of our children that Mama had cancer, his mind went to the only connection with that word he knew, a movie he saw about a football player who died of cancer, called *Brian's Song*.

"Daddy, people die when they have cancer," he said.

That was a great opportunity to distinguish for him between what we know, what we imagine, and what God has said about life.

The pictures Jesus used in Scripture help us deal with hard and stressful life experiences. God uses as visual aids the ordinary, universal things of life like clay pots, chickens, rocks, ants, and the stages of family life. These commonalities teach and comfort us. Jesus used parables and descriptions to teach us about his kingdom, to move us from the known to deal with the seemingly obscure, uncontrollable, and distant. Those areas that arouse fear in all of us.

Solace in Scripture

The tangible helps us deal with the intangibles, those horrid what ifs. I'm thankful for the Sunday school teachers who placed Bible phrases in my mind through stories, hymns, choruses, and memorized passages so that they could be stored until they were needed. On the way home from the doctor's office with the final word that yes, indeed, I had fairly advanced breast cancer, God brought to my thoughts simple concepts from the book of Psalms. I remembered my grandfather reading Psalm 91 as he and my grandmother left on a cross-country trip. I grabbed my Bible and like a child, I seemed to literally live what I read.

The year prior to the cancer diagnosis, I was leading a Bible study with a group of friends. I suggested that we use the brand-new book by Philip Yancey, *Where is God When It Hurts?* as a guide. As we went through the biblical view of suffering, we noted that this was pure theory to us, because we all had healthy bodies, minds, children, and marriages, and all the daddies had good jobs. That's probably quite unusual, but that's the way it looked then. I said I thought it was a good thing, because bad things will happen to all of us, and there's nothing like being prepared.

Within two years, one of our group was working at an entry-level job after her husband was laid off, children rebelled to varying degrees, and I was dealing with cancer. Paul uses the phrase, "and such as is common to man" regarding temptation, but all kinds of problems are common to man all over the world, in all generations. As long as we are followers of Christ in a fallen world, it's not *if* but *when* trials and tribulations will come upon us.

How am I going to read the Bible? Should I look up the word "fear" in the concordance at the back of my Bible? Or should I just read on in whatever system I happen to be using at the moment?

It doesn't make any difference. The God who knows you and me inside and out is aware of our needs and can speak to us through the process of spending time in the Word. Sometimes I cannot articulate a specific verse which answers my specific problem. I read the passage for the day, and sensed that God had spoken. "Whether you turn to the right or to the left, your ears will hear a voice behind you, saying, 'This is the way; walk in it'" (Isaiah 30:21). He was there with me, and would see me through. I felt my scattered, wild thoughts come under the control of the Holy Spirit, calming me down. Like the Apostle Paul, I often "cast down imaginations and every high thing that exalts itself against the knowledge of God, and bring into captivity every thought to the obedience of Christ" (2 Corinthians 10:5). It's an actual exercise to be acted upon. It's something that we need to do.

What does the Bible say about being scared?

The Bible does not just contain feel-good concepts to calm us down. It is the on-target, authoritative, all-sufficient guide book that gives us orientation in the major areas of human experience. The universality of human experience never changes. The Bible is filled with stories of people who experienced our fears. They were complex personalities working out the issues of fear versus faith and trust in God. Just like us.

Calm in the storm

In the northern part of the Holy Land, surrounded by agriculturally fertile hills and valleys, the Sea of Galilee sparkles like a blue jewel below the Mount of Beatitudes. The Galilee was populated with many different kinds of fish. For the people of Capernaum and surrounding villages, their lives centered around Kinneret, as the Hebrews called the large inland sea. It was the source of their livelihood. The Galilee is the main source of water for the state of Israel, then and today.

The cradle of Christianity, the Sea of Galilee is the area where Jesus centered his ministry, preaching from one fishing village to another, telling truths in parables, curing the sick, and working miracles. It was from this area that Christ gathered his followers. Usually peaceful, one night the Sea of Galilee was the cause of great fear for these fishermen turned disciples.

After Jesus fed the five thousand, he immediately made his disciples get back into the boat and cross the lake while he went into the hills alone to pray. That night, the disciples were in trouble:

The boat was already a considerable distance from land, buffeted by the waves because the wind was against it.

During the fourth watch of the night, Jesus went out to them walking on the lake. When the disciples saw him on the lake, they were terrified.

"It's a ghost," they said, and cried out in fear.

But Jesus immediately said to them: "Take courage! It is I. Don't be afraid."

"Lord, if it's you," Peter replied, "tell me to come to you on the water."

"Come," he said.

Then Peter got down out of the boat, walked on the water and came toward Jesus. But when he saw the wind, he was afraid and, beginning to sink, cried out, "Lord, save me!"

Immediately Jesus reached out his hand and caught him. "You of little faith," he said, "why did you doubt?"

And when they climbed into the boat, the wind died down. Then those who were in the boat worshipped him, saying, "Truly you are the Son of God."

MATTHEW 14:24–33

Initially bold when he asked Jesus to call him out to walk upon the water, Peter was scared to death when he took his eyes off Christ and focused them on the raging waves. We become fearful when we take our eyes off Jesus and focus them instead on the tumult besieging us. Our fears become idolatry when we are more attentive on them than on our Lord.

We all experience the storms of life. And how quickly the storms come upon us. Some are symbolic storms involving relationships, circumstances, and health. Some are real, like the storm the disciples faced that early morning between the hours of 3 and 6 a.m. It was lonely out on the sea. It was dark and dangerous. They were straining at the oars. The wind was against them. They were frightened and frenzied. They thought they might drown. No wonder, when they saw Jesus walking out to them, they thought he was a ghost.

Jesus led them into the storm. Christ has the power to find us in our storm. He has the power to calm the storm. He has the power to calm us in the storm. He can make this storm calm enough to handle or make me strong enough to handle the storm. People do not drown by falling into the water. People drown by staying there. Reach for him. He's within reach. Actually, he's reaching for us.

First things first

The trouble with fear is that it takes on a life of its own. Fear discolors the truth. While I was ill, I had to remind myself of what was fact. I had breast cancer but I was not dead yet!

Our greatest fears frequently have to do with our health and our bodies. Those cancer years taught me who the real me is. Quiet times of prayer and

140

communion connect me to God. The Word of God speaks peace to my soul.

I know no better place to flee with our fears than to the Word of God. The God who knit you together knows you inside and out and is aware of your needs. He will speak to you through the process of you spending time reading the Bible. There are so many resources *about* the Word that we run the risk of seldom dealing with the actual words and thoughts of God. I ought to know for sure what God has said and then treat all other auxiliary sources as nudges toward the truth and freedom found in God's words. There are many fine resources about the Word (like this book), but there is no substitute for the pure Word of God for washing away our fears.

The person who best exhibited this to me was my mother-in-law, Dona Matilde, who is now with the Lord. Her life verse was, "Seek first his kingdom and his righteousness, and all these things will be given to you as well" (Matthew 6:33; Luke 12:31). She was a widow with seven children, and they sometimes did not have food for the next meal. They owed nine or ten months' rent, and they were facing their furniture being put out on the street. She would simply say, "God promised that if we seek the kingdom first..." "First" for her was not a chronological thing. It meant first in prominence. Her desire. She lived for God. She honored God, and believed his Word. Her life of faith is reflected in her children.

When Luis was ten years old, his father died. The large family's living conditions slowly went downhill.

Several of the seven children were in boarding school. It was difficult for his mother to keep the construction business profitable and meet all the needs of the growing children. They moved to another city to make a new start. Luis remembers that one evening his mother told them that there was not enough food for the next evening's meal. It was not unusual for the family to eat a simple meal of a roll flavored with garlic spread, and a slice of tomato. They got on their knees and asked God to provide not just their daily bread but the long-overdue rent money.

The following day the postman brought a letter from their hometown in the province of Buenos Aires. It read, "Dear Mrs Palau, Do you remember when you were selling off the equipment from your late husband's business? I bought a tractor from you and told you that the block was cracked and that I wouldn't pay much for it, because it was practically useless. There was nothing wrong with that tractor, and for some reason, I just can't forget that I cheated a widow with orphaned children. Here's the $700 I owe you."

It is his pleasure to give us his kingdom. Romans 8:32 says, "He who did not spare his own Son, but gave him up for us all – how will he not also, along with him, graciously give us all things?"

Where is your heart? It is an uneasy question. To seek the kingdom first gives us an absent-mindedness about the world around us. I have a heart for those who have never heard about Jesus. I hear stories of people who say, "With such good news, why didn't

142

we hear of this earlier?" Those events are moving and touching. But in our mentality, with all the rainy dark clouds that float over our heads, we say, "Well, when we take care of what's up close, then we can take care of what's out further."

I believe it is the opposite. God will meet your needs here and now. Focus your vision further out. Because you are being obedient unto the ends of the earth, God will meet your needs. The healthiest church is the one who has the burden for those who have never heard about Christ way out there, as well as for those in their own community. There is room for both, but if I had to make the choice, I think that self-esteem is best served by serving, and serving as far out as possible. Oswald Chambers said, "Self-esteem is found in service." I don't have time to think about the quirkiness of my own mental processes if I am obsessed by the needs of the young women and children in India. The more I focus on others, the more my own struggles and inner turmoil are containable and under control.

This is not escaping reality. I'm well aware of what's going on right up close. But I was designed by God with the capacity to deal with the close at hand and be focused to the ends of the earth. By living in the bigger picture, occasionally I look back absent-mindedly and realize that what had previously appeared overwhelming is now something I haven't thought about, worried over, in ages.

Anchor your heart

There are certain chronic conditions we get as we grow older. I finally get to the point when the doctor says, "There's nothing I can do." The more I get busy, especially with the needs of other people, the less I notice my own aches and pains. In the end, it's better to be occupied with God's activities and more relaxed about the things that are up close.

Occasionally I find myself bothered and worried, just wanting to share it, share it, and share it – my problems, that is. It makes me boring and people start to give me a very wide berth. When we cherish our worries, they become our identity, our claim to fame, and we fear we would be lost without them. It's who we are.

When God's pleasure meets our treasure, we are on the right track. Moving from a whining heart to a heart that leans on the Lord's great goodness comes one day at a time as we learn to trust.

Anchor your heart to the steadfastness of the promises of the Lord. Make it a daily habit to read the Bible and commit verses to memory. Stuart Briscoe said, "Don't put your head on the pillow until you've first put your head in the Bible." When life is motoring along nicely in between rugged times, we tend to believe this is our right as Christ-followers. Smooth sailing.

But in his graciousness, the Lord has told us, "In this life you will have trials…" Now that's a promise. The cancer I experienced is not the only crisis that

144

has overshadowed my life. It was a big one, to be sure. I've faced, and will continue to face, challenges in terms of relationships, finances, health, and assorted problems common to man. We are on a battleship with orders to occupy it until Jesus returns. The luxury cruise comes later.

No one wants to think about a future day of adversity or testing. Living in fear of the days to come is not productive or biblical. It is a waste of the life God has given. We won't be taken by surprise if we are intimate with the Lord and his Word. "Therefore, take up the full armor of God, that you may be able to resist in the evil day, and having done everything, to stand firm" (Ephesians 6:13, NASB). Forewarned is forearmed.

It will come to us. That thing we dread. Is it unhealthy to sit around and play mental games with the what ifs of our lives? Well, yes, it could be unhealthy, if it is accompanied by a dread that clouds and changes our daily lives today. In other words, if today I modify my behavior in light of vague possibilities out there.

There are two kinds of worries. One is clear, definite, bounded by time and extremely detailed. The other is vague and undefined, difficult to explain, but very real to me. The first situation leaves me free to act, investigate, and make a plan. The second is like the comic-strip character who always wanders through life with a little black cloud over his head.

God speaks clearly, with an action plan. Our enemy loves to leave us with a nagging, unsubstantiated, unbalanced sense of paralysis. I cannot resolve, or trust God for those things I do not understand or cannot articulate.

Quite a few years ago, Luis and I ministered at a summer conference where we spent quite a bit of time with a young woman who had been born in Asia, of an Asian mother and a military father. During her growing-up years, family religious influences resulted in troubling experiences which were demonic and fearful. She found Christ as Savior, married a godly young man from a strong Christian home, and became the mother of four beautiful children.

However, at times, especially at night, dark and foreboding thoughts flooded her mind and left her emotions raw. She longed to be free. As we reviewed the promises of God with her, she understood that the power of the Lord breaks generational patterns and releases us from the sins of the fathers. The evil one is a defeated foe for the Christian. Five years later she wrote to us:

> As I u. s having my quiet time this morning
> I came across 1 John 4:4. The verse was
> highlighted and underlined. Next to it was
> noted, "Aug. 1999 – Palaus." I thought, "Wow!"
> Thanks again, for helping me to be truly set
> free through God's Word. I'm not saying Satan
> doesn't still try to control me with fear from
> things in the past, but I just say the verses you
> showed me, and he has to flee. It still brings
> tears to my eyes, being truly set free. Thank you
> for understanding and believing the things I

experienced. But mostly for showing me certain verses so I could really see God's Word.

"You, dear children, are from God and have overcome them, because the one who is in you is greater than the one who is in the world" (1 John 4:4). We are indwelt by the God of all the universe!

Powerful promises

There's nothing wrong with an academic journey into what is very real, but as yet not experienced. The intelligent discussion stalls off the "Why me?" approach. I would prefer to have an academic understanding of the guidelines of Scripture prior to a crisis.

Several years after my surgery and treatment, I received a request to visit a patient in our local hospital awaiting surgery for colon cancer. Returning to the site of my traumatic experience brought the memories flooding into my thoughts. I marched up there before I lost courage or dreamed up an excuse not to go. I found the young couple tense and nervous. I recalled how I had leaned on the Lord when I was lodged in a similar room in the same hospital. I mentioned that the Bible had been a source of comfort to me. The husband held the hospital's Gideon Bible in his hands. He absent-mindedly thumbed through the pages. "Yes," he said, "the answer must be in here someplace."

Ray Stedman said, "Woe to the man who has

to learn principles in a time of crisis." I am grateful that when my crisis came, I had already learned the principles of who God really is. When the crunch came, I had his resources firmly in mind. I could move from theory to experience. I used to answer questions at my women's Bible class in this way:"Let's battle our way through that one and try to find a rationale *now*, while we're relatively at peace, because some day, when disaster strikes, we won't be."

God is always available to us, but the problem is that in a crisis situation, surrounded by our own fear and that of others, we find it difficult to concentrate. "For the Lord comforts his people and will have compassion on his afflicted ones,"(Isaiah 49:13). I have the privilege of getting to know God and his ways when I am not under pressure so that I might endure hardship in a godly manner. It will not eliminate fear, but it will give a healthy perspective. It will answer the ultimate what ifs. My mind may reel with shock, but it will quickly shift into the reassuring promises throughout the Bible of God's presence when I know and have memorized those passages.

During the weeks Luis and I awaited an official diagnosis, we prayed for God's will to be done. We hoped he would answer that prayer by allowing us to look back on those weeks as merely a bad dream. In the past, a crisis came and it ended fast. But the final medical verdict was a malignant tumor requiring surgical removal. The news devastated us.

Long ago, I decided to lean on God's great promise to be *with* me. My cancer diagnosis came at the worst of all times – during preparations for the Spanish crusade in Los Angeles. This event was the culmination of a long-time dream for our family and ministry. Luis had to leave as I was recuperating from surgery. Fearful thoughts haunted my mind and my emotions became gloomy: "What is my family going to do without me?" and "I'm not going to be here at this time next year."

I countered the negativity by singing a praise song, and clinging to the Bible's fantastic imagery of God's love:

- "Hide me in the shadow of your wings" (Psalm 17:8).

- He is my rock, my shield, a strong tower, and my comfort. "From the ends of the earth I call to you, I call as my heart grows faint; lead me to the rock that is higher than I. For you have been my refuge, a strong tower against the foe" (Psalm 61:2–3).

- "The eternal God is your refuge, and underneath are the everlasting arms" (Deuteronomy 33:27).

- "He is your shield [defense] and helper and your glorious sword [offense]" (Deuteronomy 33:29).

Praying for others and receiving the prayers of others on my behalf is another powerful aspect of prayer.

*I have hidden your word in my heart
that I might not sin against you.
Praise be to you, O Lord;
teach me your decrees.
With my lips I recount
all the laws that come from your mouth.
I rejoice in following your statutes
as one rejoices in great riches.
I meditate on your precepts
and consider your ways.
I delight in your decrees;
I will not neglect your word.*

PSALM 119:11–16

Here are some helpful practical points:

• Spend time daily reading the Bible. Scripture brings tremendous comfort and peace.

• Highlight verses that touch your heart, especially the ones that talk about the goodness and sovereignty of God.

• Memorize passages to repeat when fear threatens your peace. Rest on those familiar passages that you've quietly thought through in times of peace.

• Look up the word *fear* in the concordance of your Bible. Search out the verses during your study of the Bible.

• Look up the word *courage* in the concordance.

Search out the verses during your study of the Bible.

• Bank on the promise of God's presence.

Good gifts

Some suggest that the words of Scripture are not an appropriate gift to give to those who hurt and are afraid. They charge it is inconsiderate, pushy, invasive, and ramming the Bible down another's throat. Certainly there are insensitive souls who constantly bump into others without any ability to assess if this is the time, the subject, or the place. Typically the insensitive one is consistently insensitive in every area, not just when wielding Scripture. Those of us who are careful, tentative, and ask permission, need not fear that it is the words of Jesus which offend.

I remember clearly who quoted what scripture to me. My soul had very sensitive antennae in those days. Sometimes, I wrote down the Bible references. Words of sympathy are long forgotten but the Word of God stays with me. Why would that be? After all, isn't it just words? No, it is the Living Word of God which speaks directly to my spirit and says, "This is truth and life affirming." And, I praise God for those who shared in any way with me. They dared to step into an uncomfortable place. Perhaps, they had no personal experience at all with life-threatening illness, let alone cancer.

We don't have to be part of an afflicted family to

lean in and contribute a good word of compassion. You don't even have to excuse your distance from the circumstances. As is commonly said, "It's the thought that counts!"

In my times of fear and uncertainty, it is *only* the Scriptures which give me perspective and some sense of where to go next. In the weeks following surgery and during the chemotherapy treatments, I spent a great deal of time looking at Bible promises. I was looking for a verse that said, "Lo, I will get you out of this mess. Quickly, and with no bad memories." I looked and looked for this verse. In case you don't already know, there is no such passage or idea in the Bible. It doesn't exist. Reading through the Bible was good for me. "I will bring you home again" (Jeremiah 27:13, NLT).

Scripture holds the high place in healing our fears. The Bible, over all other sources, is our help. The decisive confirmation in times without light is to have the words of God coincide with the words of a godly friend. What peace that brings.

For parents, final, parting words are extremely important. Before leaving on a trip, Luis and I would think of the most important thing we did not want our four boys to forget. You know that most parent-talk goes right over their heads. I suppose it should have been, "You know how much I love you," but it was probably more along the lines of "Don't pester your brother," or "Feed the cat."

Our Savior knows what we are like. His last statement to us holds utmost significance. Most of it addresses the theme of our lives – taking the Good News to those who haven't heard. The second aspect reminds us to "teach them to obey everything I have commanded you..." That's central to dealing with the fears that plague us. One of his commands is to "Fear not."

And, when the going is hard, which he above all others understood, we should remember that he closed his final instructions with the ultimate reassurance: "I will be with you always, to the very end of the age."

I know what the end of the age means technically, but I also know what it means to me in a very personal, "now" sense. Jesus promises to be with you and me, all the way to the end of the fear that plagues us. We are never alone in the battle. To the degree that the fear is overwhelming, his presence is real to a greater degree.

I have always yearned for absolute, very precise promises. Promises that unconditionally provide a quick, clean exit from the fear of the moment. When cancer invaded my body, I focused on what I knew, or thought I knew, about the ways of God.

I quickly concluded that the greatest promise from the mouth of the Lord Jesus to his followers was precisely, "I will be with you, even to the end of your resources, and the last word in bad news." That's all I need to know. I thank God for the privilege of being indwelt by the Creator of the universe. He is all I need.

In my collection of greatest encouragements from friends and believers as I worked through cancer treatment, there were an overwhelming number of versions of the same verse. Those who sent it, thought carefully in choosing it. The Holy Spirit who indwelt them brought this thought to their minds, which they passed on to me. God was speaking to me through them. Over and over, I was given Jeremiah 29:11: "'For I know the plans I have for you,' says the Lord. 'They are plans for good and not for disaster, to give you a future and a hope'"(NLT).

God did give me a future and a hope. Scripture is the very Word of the living, personal God. It is a living gift to give to those who are scared to death. Even when the frightened one is yourself. Scripture is the very Word of a living God who loves you and me deeply. It is appropriate to gently hearten a frightened sojourner by placing their trembling hand into the strong and guiding hand of the Lord by anchoring them to those passages in God's Word that comfort, strengthen, and *encourage*. There are four things you can share:

> • The tremendous comfort and peace which
> Scriptures bring, especially the portions you
> put to memory.

> • The goodness and sovereignty of God.

> • The promise of his presence.

> • The reality of the body of fellow believers
> who will pray for you, and offer practical deeds
> of love as we help bear one another's burdens.
> "Carry each other's burdens, and in this way
> you will fulfill the law of Christ"(Galatians

6:2). God puts us in group therapy – the local church.

The promises of God are given to encourage us. They are not explanations. God did not explain things to Job, but he did give his faithful servant promises. Rather than chafe at the explanations he did not get, Job clung to the promises he did receive, and those kept him going. God knows what we need. We do not need an explanation from the Creator of the universe. We do need a revelation of God. To see how great God is. Through this, we recover our perspective on life.

The power and person

After Jesus' friend Lazarus died, Jesus journeyed to Mary and Martha. "If you had been here, my brother would not have died," Martha said (John 11:21). Ifs are what hurt us and tear us apart. Like Martha, when we focus on *if*, we are not focused on the power and person of Christ. When we say "Lord," he arrives with comfort and brings healing. Jesus comforted Martha with the words, "I am the resurrection and the life. He who believes in me will live, even though he dies; and whoever lives and believes in me will never die" (John 11:25–26).

From birth to death, we deal with our fears. The person of Jesus is the answer to our fears. But to go from what we know by teaching to what we regularly experience, that is the purpose of the events of living. I secretly pat myself on the back for the fears I do not have, and never did have, but find it difficult to face the ones that have always plagued me. My prayer is that the years of knowing the Savior have made the stranglehold of fear weaker, and the time spent working through the issues is lessened.

"I've felt this way before," I tell myself, "and I'm not going to camp out here and dwell on this misery."

A little time looking at the passages of Scripture that God used to teach me to live peacefully in the midst of turmoil, eases the controlling and debilitating hold of fear and strengthens my confidence in my source – my God and his Word.

> "... O our God, will you not judge them? For we have no power to face this vast army that is attacking us. We do not know what to do, but our eyes are upon you."
>
> All the men of Judah, with their wives and children and little ones, stood there before the Lord.
>
> Then the Spirit of the Lord came upon Jahaziel son of Zechariah, the son of Benaiah, the son of Jeiel, the son of Mattaniah, a Levite and descendant of Asaph, as he stood in the assembly.
>
> He said, "Listen, King Jehoshaphat and all who live in Judah and Jerusalem! This is what the Lord says to you: 'Do not be afraid or discouraged because of this vast army. For the battle is not yours, but God's. Tomorrow march down against them. They will be climbing up

*by the Pass of Ziz, and you will find them at
the end of the gorge in the Desert of Jeruel. You
will not have to fight this battle. Take up your
positions; stand firm and see the deliverance
the Lord will give you, O Judah and Jerusalem.
Do not be afraid; do not be discouraged. Go out
to face them tomorrow, and the Lord will be
with you.'"*

2 CHRONICLES 20:12–17

APPLICATION POINT

1. What keeps you from spending daily time in
the Scriptures?

2. What step will you make today to spend
regular time in the Bible?

STEPPING OUT

Develop an insatiable biblical curiosity to know for
yourself what God said in his Word. Dive deep into the
Scriptures. Consider enrolling in a meaty Bible study,
or take a course from a seminary, not necessarily to
fulfill some educational requirement or professional
advancement, but as was said of Mount Everest,
"because it's there!"

I think for serious Bible study there is nothing
better than *Precepts* by Kay Arthur and the Bible Study
Fellowship founded by Wetherell Johnson. Both of

157

these courses are available internationally. Presently, along with friends in my local church, I am studying 1 and 2 Peter with Kay Arthur. It is a good deal of work, but the satisfaction of learning something new or getting a better understanding of something that has always perplexed me is incredibly gratifying. None of us are ever too old. I'm the visual aid for that statement. There are women in my class older than me, would you believe? One of the wonders of God's Word is that none of us will ever know it all. Even familiar parts hold new discoveries for us.

My daughters-in-law, right along with their little ones, are Bible Study Fellowship students and leaders. I am very proud of them.

CHAPTER 9

THE GOOD SHEPHERD

Savior, like a Shepherd lead us,
Much we need thy tender care.
In thy pleasant pastures feed us;
For our use Thy folds prepare.
Blessed Jesus, blessed Jesus,
Thou hast bought us, Thine we are.
Blessed Jesus, blessed Jesus,
Thou hast bought us, Thine we are.

We are Thine, do Thou befriend us,
Be the guardian of our way.
Keep Thy flock, from sin defend us;
Seek us when we go astray.
Blessed Jesus, blessed Jesus,
Hear Thy children, when they pray.
Blessed Jesus, blessed Jesus,
Hear Thy children, when they pray.

ATTRIBUTED TO DOROTHY A. THRUPP

*The Christ you have to deal with is not a weak
person outside you, but a tremendous power
inside you.*

2 CORINTHIANS 13:3–4, J. B. PHILLIPS

On a clear morning in Israel's modern-day Negev, a shepherd leisurely herds fleecy sheep across dry, rock-strewn hills to a patch of green grass splayed in a valley like a welcome mat. Intimately familiar with the few and scattered places where occasional small patches of foliage sprout, depending on the amount and frequency of rain, this is a favorite of the shepherd's because of the ancient well at the base of the low hill on the valley's east side.

In this land of Christ's nativity and where he grew in favor with God and man, the terrain is predominantly desert. Water is a valued commodity. The level of the Sea of Galilee is a constant indicator of the availability of water to the inhabitants of this pivotal piece of real estate. The flow of the Jordan River, and further south, the volume of the Dead Sea (residents call it the Salty Sea), spell security when they are full and cause for concern when less than abundant.

Satisfied that his charges are busily filling their bellies, the shepherd gathers and stacks cantaloupe-size limestone rocks, one on top of another, until the roughly circular pen is waist high. He stops frequently to allow the gentle breeze to cool his loose-fitting clothing and dry the sweat that gleams on his sun-tanned skin.

At the well, the shepherd slides away the flat

stone that covers its mouth and drops a bucket into the shallow depth. Pulling the rope, he drags the filled bucket back to the top and balances it on the rock rim. Removing the scarf wrapped around his head, he filters the water through the fabric into the couch-sized stone trough adjacent to the rough well.

After quenching his own thirst, he splashes more water into the trough and guides the sheep to drink their fill. Noting the well's low water level, the shepherd carves a groove along the side of the desert hill to guide the rainwater that falls only two months of the year. Serving as a gutter, this lengthy horizontal depression will catch the rainwater as it runs off the hills and direct the flow into the ancient well.

Weary, and glad for the dropping temperature as the sun slips behind the steep desert cliffs, the shepherd guides his herd into the oblong pen he has constructed. He counts each animal as it enters the narrow doorway. One is missing. Perching atop the rock wall, he counts a second time. The sum is still one short.

Piling a few rocks across the opening, he picks up his staff and goes searching for the missing sheep. It is nearly dark when he finds the bleating lamb, lost and lonely on a rugged mountain ledge. At the sound of his voice, the errant sheep turns toward him. He lifts the sheep and carries it across his shoulders back to the pen. Depositing the tired lamb in the fold, he removes the temporary stones across the doorway. As night falls, the protector and provider lies down across the opening, using his own body to keep his charges safely inside, and predators outside, the sheepfold.

His beloved

Modern shepherds, like their historic counterparts, tend their flocks. The description of the shepherd is used forty-eight times in the Old Testament and sixteen times in the New Testament.

Our Lord never slumbers or sleeps, but carefully provides for and protects us. "I am the good shepherd," Jesus declares in John 10:11. "The good shepherd lays down his life for his sheep." I am often fearful because I have much to lose. The more we focus on what God has said about who he is and what he will be to us, the more our conscious mind is working in a direction of faith, belief, confidence, and trust. And the hidden recesses of what we're afraid of – whether it comes from our nature, from what we've learned from others, or prompted by horrific experiences in our lives – they no longer matter. Our conscious mind begins to be confident in the ability of God to take care of us.

In Scripture, God compares us to sheep. "We are his people, the sheep of his pasture" (Psalm 100:3). We never see sheep in a circus. Clever animals who can be trained to do tricks populate the circus ring. In fact, the Bible states, "We all, like sheep, have gone astray" (Isaiah 53:6). Not some of us. All of us. No exceptions. Yet, our Good Shepherd loves us silly, fearful, and sometimes stupid sheep.

And "fear not" is a gentle command. You can almost hear the tender voice of Jesus in those comforting words. When he says, "fear not, little flock," it's a very gentle demand. He knows how hard it is, "for he knows how we are formed, he remembers that we are dust" (Psalm 103:14). There are hard sayings of Jesus, but the essence of Jesus is that he loves us, that he cares about us, and when he commands something, it's because he knows it's for our own good and his glory. He's a realist.

"If it were not so, I would have told you"(John 14:2). In addition to instilling security in us, this statement reflects Jesus' steadfast, dependable character. He is saying, "I would not put you on, I would not deceive you, I would not lead you on, because I desire your best." There isn't the slightest doubt – Jesus is trustworthy! You know, if we really believed the words of the Lord deep in our hearts and we lived with that for a long, long time, we would not be worried about stuff, because we would know, "If it were not so, I would have told you plainly."

He said this on his way to the cross, where he sealed the deal with his blood. He is not prone to overblown statements. The Lord does not exaggerate. He had a destiny, something serious to do. The Father sent him to be the Savior of the world. Deity in human flesh, he went with his eyes wide open. He knew what he was doing.

> • Jesus desires to be in relationship with you and me: "The Lord is my shepherd" (Psalm 23:1).

> • As our shepherd, Jesus promises to meet all our needs: "I shall not be in want" (Psalm 23:1).

• He feeds me in green pastures (Psalm 23:2).

• He provides safety and rest: "He makes me lie down" (Psalm 23:2).

• He satisfies my thirst: "he leads me beside quiet waters" (Psalm 23:2).

• He refreshes and heals my inmost being: "he restores my soul" (Psalm 23:3).

• Safeguarding my heart, he leads me "in paths of righteousness" (Psalm 23:3).

• In the valley of the shadow of death, during those frightening times in life, I will fear no evil, for he protects me (Psalm 23:4).

• He is always with me, showering me with the gift of his presence: "for you are with me" (Psalm 23:4).

• He directs me: "your rod and your staff, they comfort me" (Psalm 23:4).

• He provides me with food and protection: "You prepare a table before me in the presence of my enemies" (Psalm 23:5).

• He sets me apart as special to him: "You anoint my head with oil" (Psalm 23:5).

• He gives me abundance and joy: "my cup overflows" (Psalm 23:5).

• He gives me goodness and love all my days (Psalm 23:6).

• My future is secure:"and I will dwell in the house of the Lord for ever" (Psalm 23:6)."When everything is ready, I will come and get you so that you may always be with me wherever I am"(John 14:3).

Cherished by Christ

I'm inclined to think of me first. Embarrassing but true. When we take our Christmas picture, I look for my resemblance first. I judge the photo to be a good one if I look good. If I don't look good, I don't care for it. One of my daughters-in-law may say, "Well, Chris doesn't look his best in that picture." And I say, "Rats. That's too bad. He's cute, he's little. I'm old, I need all the help I can get."

Ego-centered, we look out for number one first. It's kindly called self-preservation. But I notice in John 14:3 that the Lord of the universe longs to be with us. Like a lover, he desires to keep company with his bride. He misses us. That goes all the way back to creation. Why did he create us, why did he give us free will, the ability to choose? Because this relational God doesn't want robots. He wants friends. Jesus came into the world to end our fear of death. To break the power death had over humanity. He dealt with it and he settled it on the cross. He paid our debt, and by his Spirit, now he comes to dwell within us to empower us to live successfully, boldly, courageously.

Scripture tells us that Christ bore our griefs and carried our sorrows. Isaiah 53 (the famous "Suffering

Savior" passage) gives us a description of our Good
Shepherd:

> *He grew up before him like a tender shoot,*
> *and like a root out of dry ground.*
> *He had no beauty or majesty to attract us to him,*
> *nothing in his appearance that we should desire him.*
> *He was despised and rejected by men,*
> *a man of sorrows, and familiar with suffering.*
> *Like one from whom men hide their faces*
> *he was despised, and we esteemed him not.*
> *Surely he took up our infirmities*
> *and carried our sorrows,*
> *yet we considered him stricken by God,*
> *smitten by him, and afflicted.*
> *But he was pierced for our transgressions,*
> *he was crushed for our iniquities;*
> *the punishment that brought us peace was upon him,*
> *and by his wounds we are healed.*
> *We all, like sheep, have gone astray,*
> *each of us has turned to his own way;*
> *and the Lord has laid on him*
> *the iniquity of us all.*
> *He was oppressed and afflicted,*
> *yet he did not open his mouth;*
> *he was led like a lamb to the slaughter,*
> *and as a sheep before her shearers is silent,*
> *so he did not open his mouth.*
> *By oppression and judgment he was taken away.*
> *And who can speak of his descendants?*
> *For he was cut off from the land of the living;*

for the transgression of my people he was stricken.
He was assigned a grave with the wicked,
and with the rich in his death,
though he had done no violence,
nor was any deceit in his mouth.
Yet it was the Lord's will to crush him and cause him
to suffer,
and though the Lord makes his life a guilt offering,
he will see his offspring and prolong his days,
and the will of the Lord will prosper in his hand.
After the suffering of his soul,
he will see the light of life and be satisfied;
by his knowledge my righteous servant will justify
many,
and he will bear their iniquities.
Therefore I will give him a portion among the great,
and he will divide the spoils with the strong,
because he poured out his life unto death,
and was numbered with the transgressors.
For he bore the sin of many,
and made intercession for the transgressors.

Not only can I absorb strength for my struggles by looking at his character; I can also learn to rely on another mind-boggling concept. Jesus is not just an ideal to follow, a Savior who redeems – though, as the Psalm says, that would have been enough – but he is above all the one who dwells in me! By the Holy Spirit, all that he is, is mine. And yours, when you ask him to be Lord of your life. If Jesus is the light of the world, he is also the light to bring answers to my major question marks. If he is the resurrection and the life, he brings life to my days, and energy to my path. If he is the Good Shepherd, he is aware of my hurts and my wanderings. He gently nudges me back to the safety of the sheep-pen.

Other names that describe the character of Jesus include the Way, the Truth, the Life, the Word, the Vine, Savior, Christ, Son of God, the Bread of Life, the Door, our High Priest, Lord, the Lily of the Valley, the Bright and Morning Star, the Fairest of Ten Thousand, the Bridegroom, Grace, Mercy, our Salvation.

Rest from fear

Jesus invites, "Come to me, all you who are weary and burdened, and I will give you rest" (Matthew 11:28). We are stressed, alienated, isolated, and we are uncomfortable a lot of the time. To put it another way, Jesus is saying here, "Come to me, all you who are worn out and weighed down by scrambling to meet the demands of others, and I will bring quiet to your spirits. Serve me, follow me, and because I am caring and understanding, I will stop the clamoring in your souls, for what I ask of you is not a burden at all" (Matthew 11:28–30). Sometimes we feel weary and burdened because our standards are unrealistic and we are afraid of being hopeless failures.

Look at this version: "Are you tired, worn out, burned out on religion? Come to me. Get away with me and you will recover your life. I will show you how to take real rest. Walk with me and work with me. Watch how I do it. Learn the unforced rhythms of grace. I will not lay anything heavy or ill-fitting on you. Keep company with me and we will learn to live freely and lightly."

Christ does not call us to attend another class or program, but to come directly to him. We have a choice between rest and fear. We all know the meaning of stress. Fear is a merciless taskmaster. Learn to come to Jesus the Counselor for an explanation, to Jesus the Mighty God for comfort, to Jesus the Prince of Peace for rest, because he is the only one who truly meets all your needs.

The rest Jesus promises is a sense of being refreshed and alive and quieted on the inside. What or who are you afraid to forgive? Ultimate rest is forgiveness, reaffirmed on a daily basis, but settled once at the foot of the cross. "For God did not send his Son into the world to condemn the world, but to save the world through him" (John 3:17).

The cross is the pivotal point: "that Christ died for our sins according to the Scriptures, that he was buried, that he was raised on the third day according to the Scriptures, and that he appeared to Peter, and then to the Twelve. After that, he appeared to more than five hundred of the brothers at the same time" (1 Corinthians 15:3–6). This God whom we serve, this Good Shepherd died and rose again from the dead. He is alive and sits at the right hand of his Father. How wonderful that today we do not say, "Come and see where he lies," but "Come and see where he lay." Two different words. Two different worlds. He is risen. Hallelujah!

The Good Shepherd gave his life to pay the debt for our sins that we could not pay ourselves. He rose again from the dead. He proved he is God. A good God. People can empathize deeply, but we can only go so far. Jesus invites us to come daily to him for the issues of non-rest, which include fear, guilt, sin, frustration, and all the other things that define who we really are. The only one who understands perfectly is the one who made you.

The Lord's supper, participating in communion through the breaking of bread, reminds us that the ground is level at the foot of the cross. "And he took the bread, gave thanks and broke it, and gave it to them, saying, 'This is my body given for you; do this in remembrance of me'" (Luke 22:19). Each time I take the bread and the cup in my hand, I remember that I belong. As Christ followers, worldwide we are members of the family of God. Members of his flock, we are alike in that we have a common Lord and a common trust in Christ for our salvation.

Jesus Christ, our Good Shepherd, is

- near in availability (Hebrews 4:15–16);

- near in his compassion (Psalm 34:18; Isaiah 49:13);

- near in his coming back to take us home (John 14:3).

We rejoice that we are part of such an imperfect, but redeemed family. How different from other associations where people scramble for leadership, respect, or position. "Just as each of us has one body with many members, and these members do not all have the same function, so in Christ we who are many form one body, and each member belongs to all the others"(Romans 12:5).

Jesus Christ, the Good Shepherd, was equally God and man. Prior to his death on the cross, he experienced life as we experience it. He knew the joy of loving family and friends, of attending weddings, and of building things with his hands. He knew the pain of being betrayed by friends, family, and church and community leaders:

> *Therefore, since we have a great high priest who has gone through the heavens, Jesus the Son of God, let us hold firmly to the faith we profess. For we do not have a high priest who is unable to sympathize with our weaknesses, but we have one who has been tempted in every way, just as we are – yet was without sin. Let us then approach the throne of grace with confidence, so that we may receive mercy and find grace to help us in our time of need.*
>
> HEBREWS 4:14–16

Written by John, the disciple Jesus loved, the book of Revelation records the final "I Am" statement of our Savior. Our Good Shepherd is the last word on the subject: "I am the Alpha and the Omega, the First and the Last, the Beginning and the End"(Revelation 22:13).

"For you did not receive a spirit that makes you a slave again to fear, but you received the Spirit of sonship. And by him we cry, '*Abba*, Father'" (Romans 8:15).

> *Jesus, the name that charms our fears,*
> *That bids our sorrows cease.*
> *'Tis music in the sinner's ears,*
> *'Tis life and health and peace.*
>
> CHARLES WESLEY, "O FOR A THOUSAND TONGUES"

APPLICATION POINT

1. When you think of Jesus, the Good Shepherd, what images come to your mind?

2. Scripture promises that Christ is worthy of our trust. What stands in the way of you being able to fully trust your Good Shepherd?

STEPPING OUT

My grandmother led a vacation Bible school one summer with two pre-schoolers – my brother and me. We learned the "I Am"s of the Gospel of John. These statements of Jesus let us see seven aspects of his character which comfort me still today. Every need I have is captured in his character. Because of these things, I can turn to him to meet my overwhelming need of the moment.

Find all seven of the "I Am" statements in John's Gospel. Highlight and memorize them:

Who he is and who I am – the "I Am"s of John's Gospel

- 6:35: "Then Jesus declared, 'I am the bread of life. He who comes to me will never go hungry and he who believes in me will never be thirsty.'"

- 8:12: "When Jesus spoke again to the people, he said, 'I am the light of the world. Whoever follows me will never walk in darkness, but will have the light of life.'"

- 10:9: "I am the gate [door]; whoever enters through me will be saved."

- 10:11: "I am the good shepherd. The good shepherd lays down his life for the sheep." (Also 10:14.)

- 11:25: "Jesus said to her, 'I am the resurrection and the life. He who believes in me will live, even though he dies.'"

- 15:5: "I am the vine; you are the branches."

- 14:6: "Jesus answered, 'I am the way and the truth and the life. No one comes to the Father except through me.'"

CHAPTER 10

THE CALL TO COURAGE

You are my servant,
I have chosen you and have not cast you away.

ISAIAH 41:9

When I focused on cancer, it appeared so much bigger than me. Courage came when I concentrated on God, who is mightier than cancer. Perspective depends on where I put my focus. When it pours, *he reigns.*

When King Saul and his army were arrayed against the Philistines, the entire Hebrew army was scared to death of the Philistine champion, Goliath. At nine feet and nine inches tall, he was an imposing menace. For forty days, the giant came forward every morning and every night, harassing the Israelites: "This day I defy the ranks of Israel! Give me a man and let us fight each other" (1 Samuel 17:10).

Not only was his size intimidating, but Goliath wore state-of-the-art armor, while the only person on the Israelite side who had the luxury of owning armor was King Saul. "On hearing the Philistine's words, Saul and all the Israelites were dismayed and terrified"(1 Samuel 17:11).

The Israelites saw the giant and thought he was too big. David arrived, and with his vision set on God, he saw Goliath and thought he was too big to miss!

God invites us into relationship with himself."Yet to all who received him, to those who believed on his name, he gave the right to become children of God – children born not of natural descent, nor of human decision or a husband's will, but born of God" (John 1:12–13).

Without exception, each of us has eternal value. God calls us to partner with him. "Come and see," Jesus said to his disciples (John 1:39, KJV).

"Follow me," Jesus said (Matthew 4:19). After his resurrection, he met with the disciples on the shore of their beloved Sea of Galilee. Over a satisfying meal of grilled fish, Jesus reiterated to Peter, "You follow me!" (John 21:22, NAS).

His last commandment was made moments before his ascension to heaven. "Therefore go and make disciples of all nations, baptizing them in the name of the Father and of the Son and of the Holy Spirit, and teaching them to obey everything I have commanded you. And surely I am with you always, to the very end of the age" (Matthew 28:19–20). Go and tell.

Come and see, follow me, go and tell. There is a tendency to concentrate on the "thou shalt not"s. Do not steal, do not lie, do not commit murder. Doing the "do"s is vitally important and far more fun. What to do includes:

- "Love the Lord your God with all your heart and with all your soul and with all your mind" (Matthew 22:37).

- "These commandments that I give you today are to be upon your hearts. Impress them on your children. Talk about them when you sit at home and when you walk along the road, when you lie down and when you get up" (Deuteronomy 6:7).

- "Love your neighbor as yourself" (Matthew 22:39).

- "Follow me" (Matthew 4:19).

The call to follow our Lord is a call to courage. It is often a call to change. It was for nearly everyone in the Bible. The change impacted reputations, identities, careers, and lives. The disciples stopped fishing. Moses and David stopped shepherding.

Change. It's inevitable. We can embrace it or resist it. At the foundation of much of our fear, we are reluctant to embrace God's direction because we resist the change it may bring to our lives. We get comfortable surrounded by what we know and what is familiar. Change may require more effort as I learn to live in new surroundings, with different routines, unusual experiences, and fresh relationships. It can mean venturing into a place or situation I am not accustomed to. Some intrepid souls thrive on adventure, but most of us are content to be homebodies.

Go and tell. Noah took up shipbuilding and witnessed the complete change of the entire world. Abraham changed his address. Jonah journeyed to Nineveh. Paul changed his name and his trade. Each one knew the Lord ("Come and see"), had a relationship with God ("Follow me"), and received instruction regarding where they were to go and what they were to do ("Go and tell").

Obedience

Joseph, Mary's husband in the New Testament, was a picture of obedience to the voice of God:

> *Because Joseph her husband was a righteous man and did not want to expose her to public disgrace, he had in mind to divorce her quietly.*
>
> *But after he had considered this, an angel of the Lord appeared to him in a dream and said, "Joseph son of David, do not be afraid to take Mary home as your wife, because she will give birth to a son, and you are to give him the name Jesus, because he will save his people from their sins."*
>
> *... When Joseph woke up, he did what the angel of the Lord had commanded him and took Mary home as his wife.*
>
> MATTHEW 1:19–20, 24

Joseph continued to respond immediately to God's command:

> *... an angel of the Lord appeared to Joseph in*
> *a dream. "Get up," he said, "take the child and*
> *his mother and escape to Egypt. Stay there until*
> *I tell you, for Herod is going to search for the*
> *child to kill him."*
>
> *So he got up, took the child and his mother*
> *during the night and left for Egypt.*
>
> MATTHEW 2:13–14

Joseph's instant obedience left no room for fear to hinder or halt him in the course. His immediate action had a huge and positive impact on those within his circle of influence, which includes you and me thousands of years later.

Does God honor delayed obedience? Jonah knew about that. Jonah initially ran from God's call to go to the sinful city of Nineveh and call the Ninevites to repentance. In fact, he got in a boat headed in the opposite direction. God sent a great storm, and the sailors drew lots to find out who had brought on this disaster. The lot fell to Jonah, who was tossed into the sea. God sent a great fish to swallow Jonah. For three days Jonah prayed in the belly of the fish until he and God reached an understanding.

The fish conveniently vomited Jonah onto the shore near Nineveh. Jonah made quite an impression, bleached white by the stomach acid of the fish, when he entered the city and proclaimed God's message.

Though delayed, Jonah's obedience resulted in the entire city's repentance.

Of the two, however, instant obedience rather than delayed obedience was easier on the follower. There is a strong lesson to be learned from that. I can choose to make my life easier.

Our first call is to obedience. It is to trust God and trust his guidance. Fear is the antithesis of obedience to, and trust in, the Lord. Fear in this area is why we are frustrated. It is why we are not growing and progressing in our lives. It is why we are unfulfilled. We feel guilt.

"For we are God's workmanship, created in Christ Jesus to do good works, which God prepared in advance for us to do" (Ephesians 2:10). These works are the commandments he gives us in Scripture. This is the individual call he has placed on your life and on mine.

Releasing control

Letting go of fear is letting go of control. Only to find we never really were in complete control anyway. Those who are strong controllers operate from a foundation of fear. Frequently, controllers have experienced deep hurt or betrayal or both. They respond by striving to control situations, environments, and people in a desperate attempt to protect themselves from being hurt or betrayed again.

One woman coordinated the refreshments for an event. She specified exactly how sandwiches should be cut, and how many must be on each platter. When people got in line to eat, she stood at the end of the table both to direct the line and to tell everyone to be sure to take only one Styrofoam plate. Adults found her behavior annoying. Some were insulted to be told what to do in such an obvious situation. A few laughed that something so trivial was such a big deal to her. I realized her actions were a coping device for the terror she felt if she was not in control of every detail. Her life reflected the opposite of the peace Jesus promises.

Adam and Eve tried to control their surroundings after eating the forbidden fruit. They made coverings from fig leaves to cloak their nakedness and hid from God when he came to walk with them as he customarily did in the cool of the evening. We hear the grief in God's voice as he calls to Adam, "Where are you?"

"I heard you in the garden," Adam answered, "and I was afraid because I was naked; so I hid" (Genesis 3:10).

Following their life-changing and history-changing disobedience, their first expressed emotion was fear. They ran from God. How often in our fear do we do likewise? Run from God rather than run to him? Run from relationship with the very one whose perfect love for you and me casts out fear. God's love is not based on whether I pleased him today. His love is unconditional.

Trust, the absence of fear, is essential to an intimate relationship with God:

As the Father has loved me, so have I loved
you. Now remain in my love. If you obey my
commands, you will remain in my love, just
as I have obeyed my Father's commands and
remain in his love. I have told you this so that
my joy may be in you and that your joy may be
complete. My command is this: Love each other
as I have loved you. Greater love has no one than
this, that he lay down his life for his friends. You
are my friends if you do what I command.

JOHN 15:9–14

God loves us perfectly, which is why we go to him for the resolution to our fears. Because we are being made perfect in his love over time, remnants of fear co-exist with that divine love. When I love God, the reverse is also true. Loving God, trusting him, obeying him, begins to drive out fear. It gives me the courage to come and see, follow, and go and tell. Perfect love, his love for me, equips me to obey and trust him when he beckons me to change.

Humility paves the way for faith and trust in God. I submit my will. I release my control. I put aside my pride. I recognize his lordship in my life and destiny. For those of us who habitually do things our way, humility initially is an unfamiliar path to travel.

I have learned two truths about being in control and about the love of God: (1) I don't have to be perfect; (2) I don't have to be strong all the time.

When I'm fearful, running to God, rather than away from him, opens the door to relationship with the lover of my soul and opens the door for him to bless me and fill me with the Holy Spirit, who generously grants guidance. Often I resist God's call in my life, I resist obedience, because I am afraid of what the next step may be. I'm afraid to change, to follow where he will lead me. It may be out of my comfort zone. Like Abraham, Daniel, and Joseph, it may mean relocation. For Deborah, Esther, and Gideon, it meant stepping into leadership. As it did for Moses, Peter, John, and Paul, it could mean a shift in employment. I resist obedience because I resist change.

A common first reaction to what we don't know or understand is fear. I may fear the unknown, but there is no unknown to God.

A life of significance

Fear holds me back from living a significant life, a missional life. "This is what the Lord Almighty says, 'Give careful thought to your ways. Go up into the mountains and bring down timber and build the house, so that I may take pleasure in it and be honored,' says the Lord" (Haggai 1:7–8). God called Haggai when he was eighty years old to assemble the people and rebuild the temple of the Lord. A life lived doing anything other than what God calls us to do is a dissatisfied life.

We know when we are following Christ. The evidence is that we bear fruit. "This is to my Father's glory, that you bear much fruit, showing yourselves to be my disciples" (John 15:8). "But the fruit of the

Spirit is love, joy, peace, patience, kindness, goodness, faithfulness, gentleness and self-control" (Galatians 5:22). When we are in bondage to fear, these fruits are not evident in our lives.

Failure can be success at things that don't matter. "Forgetting what is behind and straining toward what is ahead, I press on toward the goal to win the prize for which God has called me heavenward in Christ Jesus" (Philippians 3:13–14). When I am too fearful to trust God's leading, I will experience frustration and a lack of fulfillment and satisfaction. Spiritual maturity is recognizing the voice of our Good Shepherd and following God's nudging.

Following God's call doesn't mean we won't experience opposition. Our own fear is the first opposition to stand in our way. When you and I put that aside, we run smack into conflict from other sources. "In this world you will have trouble. But take heart! I have overcome the world" (John 16:33). God tests us, Satan tempts us.

When we come face to face with conflict, we are not alone. Everyone in the Old and New Testaments experienced opposition. Consider the conflict that characterized the homes of Isaac, Jacob, Samuel, and David – men who were very clearly called by God. In the New Testament, Jesus was led by the Holy Spirit into the wilderness, where he was tested by God and tempted by Satan. While all humans since Adam and Eve have failed, Jesus passed the physical, spiritual, and psychological temptations. Deep in the heart of the trials and temptations, he responded with the heart of the matter – with Scripture.

When I'm tempted to allow fear to dictate my response to God's call, I can follow Christ's example and respond with God's Word. "And God is faithful; he will not let you be tempted beyond what you can bear. But when you are tempted, he will also provide a way out so that you can stand up under it" (1 Corinthians 10:13). Why do I fear when the resources of the Father are mine – his name and all that implies, including twenty-four-hour access to him and a securely promised heritage? "I can do everything through him who gives me strength" (Philippians 4:13).

The biblical phrase, "Be of good courage," sometimes has signified to me that a chance to be brave is in my future. Hardship is on its way. But what does "good courage" mean? I believe God is saying, "Don't just have courage, but God's good courage." Experience teaches that some situations require courage without self-pity. Courage full of trust in an omnipotent God. Fear may be present but his peace is omnipresent. The admonition to be of good courage changes from something ominous to a challenge with a promise.

God's call to courage requires that I take my eyes off what I fear and off my fear itself. Like David, when I fix my eyes on God, my giant becomes too big to miss.

"My grace is sufficient for you" (2 Corinthians 12:9a), and in my weakness, he is strong, "for my power is made perfect in weakness" (2 Corinthians 12:9b). It is a tremendous relief to release my fear that the universe won't continue to be operational without me. My reassurance is in the New Testament concept of grace. Because of the work of Christ on the cross and my position in Christ, I do not get what I deserve – wrath. Instead, I receive what I don't deserve – mercy.

> *No believer should let fear of failure prevent them from responding fully to the call of God. Everything needed for life and godliness has been provided and is immediately at work in every believer that obeys God's call.*
>
> HENRY BLACKABY, *CALLED AND ACCOUNTABLE*,
> NEW HOPE PUBLISHERS, 2007

APPLICATION POINT

1. When have you delayed your obedience to God? What were the consequences of that delay?

2. When have you obeyed God's call? What did that feel like and what were the outcomes of that obedience, trust, and relationship with God?

STEPPING OUT

Look over your life. Find God's initial call on your life. Surrender to it.

Chapter 11

Simple Tools to Build
Healthy Habits

Some trust in chariots and some in horses,
but we trust in the name of the Lord our God.

Psalm 20:7

The good news is we can have freedom from fear! We can have liberty from the bondage of worry and anxiety. There will be times when we are frightened, still scared to death, but it doesn't have to paralyze us.

When Luis and I returned from the mission field, I had to quickly face one of my biggest fears – driving. Actually, the car didn't bother me as long as someone else was driving. I worked hard to cover the fact that I didn't drive. When we lived overseas, it wasn't necessary for me to drive. But back in the United States, son number three needed to be driven to kindergarten. I soon ran out of friends who would do the chore for me.

In the dead of winter in Oregon, I faced the fact

that I was thirty-five years old and couldn't drive. I knew two women who learned in their sixties. I even knew a few people who weren't too bright, and they drove. I had to learn.

I enrolled in a driver's education course for middle-aged women under the instruction of an impatient, unpleasant person. I can understand his growly, nervous, negative approach. I decided I would learn fast for no other reason than to limit the time I spent in the company of the instructor.

Telling my Bible study group was a crucial step. I asked them to hold me accountable. Every week they were to ask me how I was doing. We met in my sister-in-law's home, and since she was the designated driver to get me and my brood around when Luis was out of town, she prayed most earnestly.

I did get my driver's license and with my attending angel, I have managed all these years. My deep fear of driving was conquered because: (1) I faced the problem; (2) I let others know my need; (3) I asked them to hold me accountable; (4) I faced these people on a regular basis; and (5) I cooperated with God to bring the needed outcome – the ability to drive.

While living in other cultures, I wondered if mothers in those other places on the globe feared the same things I did. Or did those women have a more fatalistic approach to sickness, danger, and threats? Did they just accept loss, even death, as inevitable or out of their control? Did they shrug it off?

Getting to know my neighbors and church friends in Latin America, in places with limited resources and certainty, I discovered that they are just like me. They don't passively accept losses and risks. They love their children and want to keep them safe and healthy. They fear old age and weakness.

Human experience has commonalities which make the words of the Bible always relevant. Geography, time, culture or race do not separate us from the common truth that stabilizes and gives us direction and peace.

God's Word contains everything we need to not merely survive, but to thrive. "I have come that they may have life and have it more abundantly," Jesus tells us in John 10:10 (NKJV). "His divine power has given us everything we need for life and godliness through our knowledge of him who called us by his own glory and goodness. Through these he has given us his very great and precious promises, so that through them you may participate in the divine nature and escape the corruption in the world caused by evil desires" (2 Peter 1:3). I participate in the divine nature. Imagine that! "For in Christ all the fullness of the Deity lives in bodily form," and we are complete in him (Colossians 2:9–10).

God's written Word gives us resources that are far superior to all of our combined wisdom over the centuries for coming to grips with our great enemy, fear, and its cousins, anxiety and worry. A gospel hymn said it well: "No one understands like Jesus."

In your reading of the Bible, notice the gentle comments and commands from the beginning to the end that say, "do not let your hearts be troubled and do not be afraid" (John 14:27), and "surely I am with you always, to the very end of the age" (Matthew 28:20). There is reassurance that God is aware of how we feel. He knows us. He remembers what we are like. God sympathizes with the natural and the unnatural fears we have, but loves us too much to leave us to wallow in those fears.

In Matthew 26 we read about Peter's incredible failure when he denied Jesus Christ three times. When Christ rose from the dead, an angel instructed the women, "But go, tell His disciples – and Peter – that He is going before you into Galilee; there you will see Him, as He said to you" (Mark 16:7, NKJV). In the same way Christ pursued Peter, he pursues us. It was Peter's intense encounter with Jesus that changed Peter from a fearful man into a dynamo for the remainder of his highly productive life. Peter denied Christ before a fire in the high priest's courtyard. Jesus brought Peter right back in front of a fire on the shore of the Sea of Galilee, where Christ affirmed his love, forgiveness, and acceptance of Peter. It is the same for us. "We love him because He first loved us" (1 John 4:19, KJV).

1 Peter 5:7 says, "Cast all your anxiety on him because he cares for you." Every word in that command counts. It shows it can be done. God's commands are his enablings. He demands a willingness to live a carefree life, and he gives his power to us because he dwells within us to make obedience possible.

Hebrews 11 lists those in God's Hall of Faith. Those spiritual greats were frightened of living life with Jesus. The truth is, life in God's family can be difficult. But they couldn't imagine life without him. It is the same for us. Life may be hard with the Lord, but I can't conceive of life without God.

But remember, it is a process. People say, "But I did pray. I did ask the Lord." Yes, and he did hear you. Begin to look for the ways he is answering your prayer. Sometimes he answers our prayers and we don't even notice.

Here are some keys to help you get free from the glass box that fear locks us in.

Pray

Put fear and worry on hold until after you've read the Word and taken your concerns to the Lord in prayer. I have developed a discipline of sitting in my old chair and giving it to God. I pray, "Lord, you are the only one who can oversee this."

What are the facts of your situation?

Write them down. Take stock of your situation and get it all out there in front of you where you can see it. Facing my fear of cancer made me a stronger woman. I wish there were an easier way.

One friend shared, "On a quiet day I read and re-read Philippians 4:6–7. As Paul tells us, I made a list of all the anxieties and fears we are facing – quite a list. By each one I added some thanksgiving, and a request concerning that anxiety. It was strengthening. The peace that Paul promises and the comfort is not always there in a felt way. I'm glad it surpasses our understanding."

What is the worst that can happen?

Look at the worst-case scenario. Differentiate between what you won't do and what you can't do. List the advantages of this precarious situation. Many successful entrepreneurs claim that losing their job was the catalyst that gave them opportunity to create their own business.

Face the facts you have just recorded

Do you have cancer? Is a family member mentally ill? Are you in an abusive situation? Analyze your options. Is there someone you can talk with who has walked this journey before you? Is there a support group in your area? Educate yourself on the topic. We are much more fearful of what we don't understand.

In the 1960s, a few brave celebrity types decided to write bluntly and honestly about their experience with breast cancer. Until then, no one talked or wrote about it. I read a long magazine article on the subject. Did it solve everything and send me fearlessly through several years of life-threatening surgeries, side-effects, and therapies? Of course not. The real thing is the real thing. However, it helped. I remember telling myself, "If that ever happened to me, I would…" Information is power.

During the years I underwent treatment, I made

a true friend in the Chicago area. Janie was just enough senior to me that I looked up to her, and we spent some great times together. One day over lunch she told me that when she was young, she also was diagnosed with breast cancer. Although grateful for a full recovery, she mourned the loneliness that came from the fact that she did not feel free to share her pain with anyone. No one knew much about breast cancer, and the experience seemed off-limits for discussion. While other ailments had respectability, this particular cancer did not.

One friend shared that her grandmother wouldn't even say the word "cancer." When the grandmother had a skin cancer removed, she whispered that she had the "'C' word, and be sure not to tell the grandchildren." Previous generations considered pregnancies and mental-health problems taboo for polite conversation. A woman in her seventies shared that she just found out she had an older brother. When the baby was born retarded, the doctor advised the family to institutionalize the child and go home and forget about him.

Ignorance compounds our fear and encourages us to pull away from others. Confusion and ignorance waste what little emotional strength we have at a time when we can ill afford to stumble around in the dark. Approach surgery, relocation, and the need for a life change in a matter-of-fact way. Get the facts. Educate yourself. Ask questions. You can better face what's ahead and what needs to be done when you know a little bit about it.

Go in spite of your fears

Sometimes you have to. A lot of scary things have to be done anyway. Gideon was scared to lead his people into battle against a fierce and intimidating enemy. But he did it anyway (Judges 6–7). Though I was scared when I was diagnosed with cancer, I had to do it anyway. There was no way to opt out or decide I'd come back to do this another day. I had to sally forth, putting one foot in front of the other. Most of us have to undergo surgery or at least a root canal sometime. Though we're frightened, we go in spite of our fear.

One friend's sister was destroying her life and harming her family through alcohol abuse. Though she was terrified of the angry backlash she expected would come from her sister, this woman got counsel from a qualified counselor, enlisted the help of extended family, and set a day for intervention. Despite her trepidation, she did what needed to be done.

Similarly, women in other countries risk serious cultural backlash to meet weekly on a rooftop for Bible study. Unable to have a Bible in their homes, these women memorize Scripture and apply God's Word to their lives. They pray for their loved ones. They are frightened of repercussions, but more frightened of an eternity without the mighty God of the universe for themselves and their families. The fellowship with other believers is worth the risk.

I have made several trips to help with a wonderful ministry to women in South India. Each visit results in a kind of cultural overload – there are so many different customs, ways to help, needs I've never encountered. I try to teach the Bible to different segments of the ministry. A different voice is good for them. The highlight is always the fortnightly meeting on a rooftop for women. About eighty women crowd quietly in and find a place to sit on the flat roof. They tearfully speak fervent prayers and recite Scripture. Memorized passages feed their souls between these clandestine meetings. It is humbling to have them correct me. Their precious Bibles are often buried in the yard and taken out only when they will not be seen by unbelieving husbands. I am bolstered in my faith by worshiping and praying with women who have persevered in their faith despite the beatings they may endure. They come at about 6 p.m., the time when they are out of the house buying food for the evening meal. These very bright, literate sisters of mine recite entire chapters which they have committed to memory. They exemplify believers who go forward despite their fears.

After my cancer surgery, a friend came to visit me in the hospital. Later, I wondered if I would have had the courage to visit someone who had just experienced the darkest day of her life. She didn't know me that well. I'm grateful she wasn't afraid to come to my hospital room. I'm grateful she wasn't afraid to care.

Courage does not always roar.
Sometimes, it is the quiet voice
at the end of the day saying,
"I will try again tomorrow."

MARY ANNE RADMACHER

Take baby steps

Choose to do the right thing, especially if you know what it is and have the capacity to do it. Establish a plan for change and make small steps of progress toward the larger goal. Accept criticism and move forward. Don't give up.

One of the major proofs of the fall of man and all creation is the difficulty of maintaining balance and perspective. We seem to leap onto a horse and gallop wildly in one direction before realizing, "Oh, goodness, that's too much." Then we find another horse and dash madly in the opposite direction. One of my constant prayers is, "Lord, help me see things as they really are."

When my friend's husband became abusive, she had to rebuild her entire life. She was terrified. She evaluated where she was and where she needed to be. She broke down the journey into steps and tackled one project at a time. She met with her pastor, a counselor, and an attorney. Next, she filed the necessary charges with the police. While maintaining regular counseling appointments for her children, she sold her house and relocated to a place she could afford by herself that was close to her children's school and their church.

In two years, this woman rebuilt her life into a positive environment where her family could thrive. Amidst emotional, physical, and spiritual turmoil, she faced her fears victoriously by leaning on the Lord and taking one baby step at a time.

Commit to living by biblical principles

Occasionally I recommit to that list of biblical priorities I wrote down on the heels of my diagnosis. How stupid it would be not to learn anything through that experience.

Love the Lord with all your heart, soul, mind, and strength. "The time is now for the important things with family, friends, and the Lord," I wrote in my journal. And the time is never for the fussy, nit-picking household things that I get bogged down in. These are the priorities taught by the Master Teacher.

Live by God's timetable

God has time. "And I am certain that God who began the good work within you, will continue his good work until it is finally finished on that day when Christ Jesus returns" (or we go to be with him!) (Philippians 1:6).

Discouragement is always in the short term. There will be days when it is difficult to put one foot in front of another. One friend's worst nightmare became reality when her husband abandoned her and her children. Six months later her brother telephoned from another state to ask how she was doing.

"Some days it hurts so bad I can't breathe," she described. "I can take an aspirin for a headache, but there isn't anything to relieve my heartache."

A year later she reported that those days of deep emotional pain were coming less frequently. "When I have a day like that now, I know it will pass. It's no longer my address. I have to walk through it because it is part of the healing process. I can't walk around it, under it, or over it. The only way is through it."

Because God is ever present, he is always with us. "Where can I go from your Spirit? Where can I flee from your presence?" (Psalm 139:7). God has all the time in the world. He has never run out of time with anyone and he is not going to begin with you and me. That takes a lot of pressure off you and me. We don't have to be perfect by the day after tomorrow.

In a notebook, record the Scripture verses and inspirational words that helped you

Write down the encouraging words others speak to you. In the Bible, search for encouraging verses. There are lots of them. Memorize God's promises. List the helpful acts people do for you that become the wind under your wings. I began such a notebook during my cancer years. Luis writes down prayer requests, verses that apply, and answered prayers with the dates.

Recently, my four daughters-in-law and I spent a night together in a cute little hotel. In doing some digging around for things I'd written in the past regarding the raising of our sons with a frequently absentee father, I found a journal I'd kept for about a year right in the middle of a lot of adolescent happenings. We read some of it together and we laughed. It's humorous now, looking back on shenanigans, but it wasn't then. The next generation is moving into the same growing-up stage with their own children, my grandchildren. It brings tears of gratitude to my eyes to see the totally loving hand of God, patiently guiding my immature children and their equally inept mother, keeping us safe. "Fear not," little Palau flock.

Return to the notebook and read it when you are plagued by gloomy thoughts

The writings in my book are my memorial of God's miracles in my life. It is like the stones God told the Israelites to pick up from the bottom of the Jordan when God parted the river and the people crossed on dry land to the other side:

> *Choose twelve men from among the people,*
> *one from each tribe, and tell them to take up*
> *twelve stones from the middle of the Jordan from*
> *right where the priests stood and to carry them*
> *over with you and put them down at the place*
> *where you stay tonight. In the future, when your*
> *children ask you, "What do these stones mean?"*
> *tell them that the flow of the Jordan was cut off*
> *before the ark of the covenant of the Lord. When*
> *it crossed the Jordan, the waters of the Jordan*
> *were cut off. These stones are to be a memorial to*
> *the people of Israel forever.*
>
> JOSHUA 4:2–3, 6–7

Practice praise

Praise the Lord aloud. Sing hymns and spiritual songs. One chorus says, "God inhabits praise." After the doctor diagnosed my cancer, I unraveled my despair by playing the piano and singing hymns that have become dear to me with lines like, "He hideth my soul in the cleft of the rock," "'Tis so sweet to trust in Jesus," and "When darkness veils his lovely face, I rest on his unchanging grace." Psalm 16:11 promises, "You will show me the path of life; In Your presence *is* fullness of joy; At Your right hand *are* pleasures forevermore" (NKJV).

A friend described her fears centered around being claustrophobic. A problem with her back necessitated MRI tests. The first ones, years ago, involved being confined in a closed, dark cylinder with loud clinking noises as the machine operated. The patient had to hold completely still during the entire test which seemed to last forever. More recently the machines have improved greatly, but this test roused a sense of dread for those who feared tight, closed-in places.

"The Lord, of course, was gracious," my friend reported. "I found myself singing hymns and choruses during the time in the tube. I sang them in my head, actually. I kept repeating my favorites and focusing on him rather than my fears. I don't know why being confined was so scary for me. Perhaps that is the way with fear – it just is, whether there seems to be a good reason or not."

Avoid triggers

Sometimes you must avoid people who cause you to fear and worry. Bound in their own fears and questions, some people are incapable of pushing you where they have never been themselves.

Some people have firmly held, immovable opinions and feel they are entitled to express them, no matter who gets hurt. Other folks sit on the fence while they figure out what they think you want to hear, then jump off the fence to make sure you understand they completely agree with you.

I have known both types of people, and it's no fun. The first type scares me to death and I give them a wide berth, because I am no master of argument. The second type will never be "as iron sharpens iron, so one man sharpens another" (Proverbs 27:17). Substitute venomous relationships with ones that inspire a closer walk with God. Simply move unhealthy relationships to an outer circle and populate your inner circle with special chosen companions. Even Jesus hand-picked his inner circle, his disciples.

Spirit-led followers of Jesus are focused on the commands of Scripture. Speaking the truth in love, they are as transparent and candid as their human frame allows. Their sense of identity reflects Romans 12:3: "Do not think of yourself more highly than you ought, but rather think of yourself with sober judgment, in accordance with the measure of faith God has given you." This is biblical self-esteem.

When fears wash over you, find the trigger. Ask yourself, "Where did this come from?" When you find yourself going down the path that leads to the bottomless pit of fear and depression, train your thoughts to take another route. "I used to go down that trail to that familiar deep hole," one woman said. "Then I learned how to go around the hole. Now I've learned not to even go down that path."

2 Corinthians 10:5 tells us to "take captive every thought to make it obedient to Christ." God clearly warns us that much of our fear can be avoided if we replace the rehearsing of fearful thoughts with the rehearsing of God's promises. When we dwell on negative thoughts, it causes death in our relationship with God. We stop trusting him. The problem looms larger and larger. As the pain increases, trust decreases.

Satan is a master at half truths. He continues today the same tactics he began in Genesis 3. "Did God really say...?" he taunted Eve in the garden (verse 1). "You will not surely die," he said, contradicting God's direct command to Adam (verse 4). The deceiver earned his name. Jesus is the Truth. "I saw heaven standing open and there before me was a white horse, whose rider is called Faithful and True" (Revelation 19:11).

For women, poor and uncontrolled thought life manifests in worry. For men, it tends to manifest in impure thoughts.

Are your thoughts noble, right, lovely, admirable, excellent and praiseworthy? Those are what God has instructed us to concentrate on (Philippians 4:8–9). Why? Because then the God of peace will be with you. He said so:

> *Let the peace of Christ rule in your hearts,*
> *since as members of one body you were called*

to peace. And be thankful. Let the word of God dwell in you richly as you teach and admonish one another with all wisdom, and as you sing psalms, hymns and spiritual songs with gratitude in your hearts to God. And whatever you do, whether in word or deed, do it all in the name of the Lord Jesus, giving thanks to God the Father through him.

COLOSSIANS 3:15–17

The world's peace is fragile, easily set off balance, under the domination of circumstances, moods, pressures, temperaments, seasons, present companions, and noise, just to name a few. God says, "Peace I leave with you; my peace I give you. I do not give to you as the world gives. Do not let your hearts be troubled and do not be afraid" (John 14:27).

Guard what you allow into your mind, what you receive in your heart. The eyes and ears are the doorways to our mind and heart, and we control what we allow to pass through. "I will set before my eyes no vile thing" (Psalm 101:3). "But the wisdom that comes from heaven is first of all pure; then peace-loving, considerate, submissive, full of mercy and good fruit, impartial and sincere" (James 3:17).

When fear steals your peace, stop and pray. As the children of Israel waited in the desert for the pillar of fire by night and the pillar of cloud by day to lead them, wait upon the Lord to lead and guide you. Right praying, right thinking, and right living is a fine solution to fear and worry.

Leave the unknown to the One who knows all things

Don't try to understand all of life's whys. Some exploration of human personality yields helpful information that enables us to function more effectively. But there are other areas of knowledge that we ought to commit to him "who has done everything well" (Mark 7:37). Those murky, unresolved subjects are fodder for great anxiety. "The Lord our God has secrets known to no one. We are not accountable for them, but we and our children are accountable forever for all that he has revealed to us, so that we may obey all the terms of these instructions." (Deuteronomy 29:29). I have more than enough clear truth to keep me busy for this lifetime.

Today many of our models, whether in the Christian life, marriage, or child rearing, are overly idealistic. They give the false expectation that as Christians, we should be able to easily and quickly arrive at certain standards. Their illustrations are not the norm, not common to you and me. Let's be honest. Thankfully, God is realistic. He wants to accomplish steady, often imperceptible growth in us day after day, month after month, year after year until we finish the course set before us. The growth of a child on a daily basis is imperceptible until you get out his growth chart and see how tall he was a year ago. That's why I like the fact that the Christian life is spoken of in terms of walking. Slow and steady.

Hebrews 12 instructs, "Run the race before you." Just ahead of us, Jesus encourages us on. Jesus is not saying, "Run faster! You're not doing a good enough job."The very thought is laughably uncharacteristic of our Lord. He perseveres with us.

Jesus persevered with the disciples to the end. How frustrating it must have been for him. During his last week on earth, prior to the crucifixion, he taught them many profound truths about serving one another and suffering for the kingdom. How did these selected men respond? They asked, "Who gets to sit on your right hand?" *Come on, men!* he must have thought. But the Lord persevered. He saw what the disciples were going to be, not just what they were at that moment. "Let us not become weary in doing good, for at the proper time we will reap a harvest if we do not give up"(Galatians 6:9).

Part of this resting in the Lord is literal. A good night's sleep, and a generally healthy pattern of sleep is essential for fearless living. When we are sleep-deprived, little worry demons float around in our heads and we have fewer resources to deal with them. How often after a good night's sleep, I either discount the fears of yesterday as out of perspective, or I find a simple solution to what plagued me the night before. I often say to my husband, "We're too tired to deal with this tonight. Let's leave it until tomorrow." A new day, a rested mind and body, and the future is brighter.

The Lord sees what you are going to be, not just what you are at this moment. His eyes are always on you. "For his eye is on the sparrow and I know he watches me," the gospel song says. Fix your eyes on Jesus. Keep everlastingly at it. You may not see instant changes, but Jesus will be changing you in his time. Your godly perseverance makes a difference for all eternity.

Is God worthy of your trust? Is he worthy to be trusted with your fears? The answer is a comforting and resounding *yes*.

> *Turn to the Lord Jesus Christ himself.*
> *Don't sit down and commiserate with yourself.*
> *Don't try to work something up,*
> *but – this is the simple essence of it –*
> *go directly to him and seek his face,*
> *as the little child runs to its father or mother.*
> *Seek Him, seek His face, and all other things shall be*
> *added unto you.*
>
> D. MARTYN LLOYD-JONES

APPLICATION POINT

1. From the list above, what is the easiest step for you to implement today?

2. What is the second easiest step you will implement next?

3. What is the goal you are aiming for? Write down the baby steps will you take to get there.

STEPPING OUT

In your Bible, highlight Scripture verses that provide comfort in the face of your fear. Begin with 2 Timothy 1:7. As you read the Bible, record your insights in the margins or in a journal.

CHAPTER 12

TALK TO GOD

This, then, is how you should pray:

"Our Father in heaven,
hallowed be your name,
your kingdom come,
your will be done
on earth as it is in heaven.
Give us today our daily bread.
Forgive us our debts,
as we also have forgiven our debtors.
And lead us not into temptation,
but deliver us from the evil one.
(For yours is the kingdom and the power and the
glory for ever.
Amen.)"

MATTHEW 6:9–13

Thank you Father, for this moment of quiet, and for
the strength
to pick up my tasks again, renewed and refreshed,

because I have paused to be with You,
for the sake of Jesus Christ our Lord.

SHERWOOD E. WIRT

Curled up in the fetal position, the last thing I feel like doing is praying. When the bottom has fallen out of my world, when my heart is broken, I don't have the strength. I don't have the faith. Yet, at this exact moment, prayer is what I most need.

Prayer is talking to God. It can be a two-way conversation as God speaks to my heart through the Holy Spirit and through his written Word in Scripture. When I can't pray, the Holy Spirit intervenes on my behalf. "We do not know what we ought to pray for, but the Spirit himself intercedes for us with groans that words cannot express. And he who searches our hearts knows the mind of the Spirit, because the Spirit intercedes for the saints in accordance with God's will" (Romans 8:26–27). Prayer is an attitude of coming into the presence of the Lord. When words won't come, it is enough that I come into his presence. Like a child who climbs up on a parent's lap to be gently enfolded in the security of safe arms, so it is when I wordlessly come into his presence and allow myself to be held. To be loved.

Other times the words come in a jumbled tumble, gushing fast and pouring upon each other in a furious flood. Sometimes, I'm reasonable and organized. Sometimes I rage, complain, and whine. There have been times when my prayers consisted of, "Oh God!"

No matter whether my prayer is a wordless sob

or a torrent of furiously spoken phrases, the Lord receives me. "The Lord your God is with you, he is mighty to save. He will take great delight in you, he will quiet you with his love, he will rejoice over you with singing" (Zephaniah 3:17). He is glad I came to him. "This is the confidence we have in approaching God: that if we ask anything according to his will, he hears us. And if we know that he hears us – whatever we ask – we know that we have what we asked of him" (1 John 5:14–15).

When I least feel like it, that's when I most need to pray. Prayer gets everything out where God and I can get a good look at my concerns. Prayer has a mysterious power to help me obey my Lord. Prayer is where I practice leaving my fears at his feet. "Call to me and I will answer you and tell you great and unsearchable things you do not know" (Jeremiah 33:3).

Paul writes: "Don't fret or worry. Instead of worrying, pray. Let petitions and praises shape your worries into prayers, letting God know your concerns. Before you know it, a sense of God's wholeness, everything coming together for good, will come and settle you down. It's wonderful what happens when Christ displaces worry at the center of your life" (Philippians 4:6, The Message).

The Old Testament outlines three components to prayer: praise, supplication, and thanksgiving. Prayer is talking to God. Praise is acknowledging who God is, recognizing that he is big enough to solve our problems. Supplication is asking intensely and honestly. Thanksgiving is expressing appreciation.

Adoration, devotion, and worship are also part of prayer. The book of Haggai outlines a formula for prayer: praise plus poise plus prayer equals peace. Such peace is the result of constant conscious communion with the Lord through prayer.

> *The time of business does not for me differ from*
> *the time of prayer; and in the noise and clatter*
> *of my kitchen, while several different persons*
> *are at the same time calling for different things,*
> *I possess God in as great tranquility as if I were*
> *upon my knees... we should establish ourselves*
> *in a sense of God's presence by continually*
> *conversing with Him.*
>
> BROTHER LAWRENCE, THE PRACTICE OF THE PRESENCE
> OF GOD

Luke's Gospel tells the story of ten lepers who came to Christ asking to be healed. Jesus was merciful and healed them. Though these ten were quick to whine about their condition and ask for healing, they were slow to thank the Lord. In fact, only one of the ten took the time to return to Jesus and give thanks (Luke 17:11–19). Too often I spout off my laundry list of complaints and requests, and neglect to voice my deep appreciation for the grace and mercy my Lord bestows on my prayers.

The Lord is near in availability and invites us into his presence. "Let us then approach the throne of grace with confidence, so that we may receive mercy and find grace to help us in our time of need" (Hebrews

4:16). Jesus invites, "Ask and you will receive, and your joy will be complete" (John 16:24).

Run to God

Why do we hesitate to pray? We fear that when we make our request to our heavenly Father, he just might say no. Harriet Beecher Stowe wrote, "I feel all the bitterness of the eternal 'no.'"

In times of grief, I pray that God will remind me of the truths I already know. When my heart pulls back from prayer because I'm afraid the great God is too busy, when my mind repeats a litany of negative what if's, I ask the Lord to remind me of his eternal promises. Also, we are incurably lazy. We feel we must be *doing* something, as though prayer is not.

God invites us to come boldly before his throne. "Rejoice in the Lord always. I will say it again: Rejoice! Let your gentleness be evident to all. The Lord is near. Do not be anxious about anything, but in everything, by prayer and petition, with thanksgiving, present your requests to God. And the peace of God, which transcends all understanding, will guard your hearts and your minds in Christ Jesus" (Philippians 4:4–7). That invitation is given by God who wants, desires, encourages us to bring our concerns directly to him.

Communicate and connect

Prayer is about communicating, not outcomes.

Why do I pray? Because the Trinity wants to talk

to me, and it blesses me too. Prayer may be worrying out loud in God's direction sometimes. Although I remember to whom I am speaking, I also feel free to let him know how things are going, my fear of the day. Does he already know it? Of course, but he is more than willing to listen and respond, because he cares about me and yearns for relationship.

During the difficult period of chemotherapy for breast cancer, I was asked to take part in the Good Friday service in our church. Recently, I came upon the notes from that little devotional. Isaiah 53 says of our Suffering Savior, "Surely, he has borne our grief and carried our sorrows." How many times I had looked at that predictive passage and focused on the awful sufferings Jesus bore on the cross for our sins. Never, until my attention was clearly on the subject because of personal pain, had I noticed that along with carrying my sins to the cross, the sinless Son of God also carried my sorrows. My sense of sorrow and loss was very close to the surface, and I could only sing with the congregation, "Hallelujah, what a Savior!" All those things that lay in the negative, the results of the fall, were there on that cross.

My friend has lupus. During her prayer time, God asked her three questions: "Do you know me?" "Do you love me?" "Do you trust me?"

"But why, Lord?" she asked.

"That's not one of the questions," was his reply.

When we can answer "Yes" to all three questions, the anxieties and fears fall back or disappear.

I cannot learn from Jesus why bad things occur, why

an avalanche or flood or fire or earthquake decimates one town and not its neighbor, why leukemia strikes a child, or cancer attacks a loved one. But the Lord assures me these events grieve his heart. Jesus wept when he witnessed the grief of his good friends Mary and Martha over the death of their beloved brother, Lazarus. He wept over the bustling city of Jerusalem when he viewed the horrors and pain in that beloved city's future. "How often I have longed to gather your children together, as a hen gathers her chicks under her wings, but you were not willing" (Matthew 23:37).

> *Prayer has become for me much more than a shopping list of requests to present to God. It has become a re-alignment of everything. I pray to restore the truth of the universe, to gain a glimpse of the world, and of me, through the eyes of God. In prayer I shift my point of view away from my own selfishness. I climb above the timberline and look down at the speck that is myself. I gaze at the stars and recall what role I or any of us play in the universe beyond comprehension. Prayer is the act of seeing reality from God's point of view.*
>
> PHILIP YANCEY,
> *PRAYER, DOES IT MAKE ANY DIFFERENCE*,
> HODDER & STOUGHTON, 2008, P. 21

Help my unbelief

Trust. Hebrews 11 records the biblical Hall of Fame – those spiritual greats who believed what was unseen. When we fear, when we don't fully trust, we are also named among the greats. If there was a Hall of Doubt, it might include "doubting Thomas," but my name would be at the top of the list. There are plenty of biblical examples of incidents of doubt on the path to trust.

John the Baptist, the cousin of Jesus, forerunner of his ministry, and the man who baptized the Son of God, sent word from prison to ask, "Are you the one or should we look for another?"

John the Baptist's father, Zechariah, a Jewish priest, was serving in the Temple when an angel appeared. "When Zechariah saw him, he was startled and gripped with fear. But the angel said to him: 'Do not be afraid, Zechariah; your prayer has been heard. Your wife Elizabeth will bear you a son, and you are to give him the name John'" (Luke 1:12–13).

Some of our favorite Christmas Bible passages are stories of fearful people encountering the divine. "Joseph son of David, do not be afraid to take Mary home as your wife," instructed the angel (Matthew 1:20). "And there were shepherds living out in the fields nearby, keeping watch over their flocks at night. An angel of the Lord appeared to them, and the glory of the Lord shone around them, and they were terrified. But the angel said to them, 'Do not be afraid. I bring you good news of great joy that will be for all the people'"

(Luke 2:8–10). These stories reassure us not only that we are not the first to grapple with fear, but also that even those who were physically closer to Jesus Christ, shared our common experience with fear.

The Old Testament shares similar stories. When the Syrian army made war against Israel, Elisha's servant was scared to death. Elisha assured him, "Do not fear, for those who are with us are more than those who are with them." Elisha prayed and God allowed his servant to see, "And behold, the mountain was full of horses and chariots of fire all around Elisha" (2 Kings 6:16–17, NKJV).

Jonah struggled to trust God when God told him to preach to Nineveh, a city known for lining the road that led to it with the dead bodies of prophets. It was an effective deterrent.

With conviction, faith, and fear, Esther directed that a fast with prayer be undertaken on her behalf before she went before the king to plead for the preservation of herself and her people.

When situations don't look like I think they should look, I question God's trustworthiness. There is a list of items and events on my life script that I don't think should be there and I'm fearful – terrified – of what he may allow or write next. I don't believe these things are for my best.

In tough times, I'm overwhelmed by questions. To make matters worse, I have questions about my questions. Is it wrong to have questions? Is it normal to have questions? Is it all right to question God? I do know God is not afraid of my questions. He invites them. "'Come now, let us reason together,' says the Lord" (Isaiah 1:18).

The Psalmist asked a lot of questions:

> • "Why, O Lord, do you stand far off? Why do you hide yourself in times of trouble?" (Psalm 10:1).

> • "How long, O Lord? Will you forget me for ever? How long will you hide your face from me? How long must I wrestle with my thoughts and every day have sorrow in my heart? How long will my enemy triumph over me?" (Psalm 13:1–2).

> • "Will the Lord reject for ever? Will he never show his favor again? Has his unfailing love vanished for ever? Has his promise failed for all time? Has God forgotten to be merciful? Has he in anger withheld his compassion?" (Psalm 77:7–9).

His questions centered around "Why?" and "How long?" When he did not get answers to his "Why?" questions, he asked the "How long?" questions. But still God did not answer. Let's get personal. Like the Psalmist, I don't always get answers to my questions. I am increasingly aware that my finiteness does not allow me to grasp the reasons for life's perplexities. I'm glad God does not give trite, easy, flippant justifications to questions that are beyond my understanding.

Can I surrender? Will I choose to allow God to be

God? Will I surrender control of my life? Do I believe he loves me and has my best in mind? Will I trust him wholeheartedly? Will I abandon myself to him? Will I trade my fear for trust?

Sometimes we need a time limit on worrisome issues. Like the man in Mark 9:24, I cry, "I do believe; help me overcome my unbelief."

Fear often manifests in anger. People asked if I went through the anger-at-God stage of the grief process when I had cancer. Dr Elisabeth Kubler-Ross developed a list of five psychological preparations for death. It was a much-discussed theory at the time. The five stages are shock or denial, anger, bargaining, depression, and acceptance. I didn't feel I needed to follow that list. I manufacture enough ways to react to problems without needing suggestions from anyone else. I make a distinction between anger against God – a defiance I believe is almost blasphemous – and the emotion of deep frustration. Taking my cues from the world and shaking my fist at God when I most need to cooperate with him isn't smart or necessary. "Everyone should be quick to listen, slow to speak and slow to become angry, for man's anger does not bring about the righteous life that God desires" (James 1:19–20).

My prayers during fearful times sound like this: "Lord, I don't like what is going on, but I know You want only good for me. I don't understand this, Father." His response is in Isaiah 53:4: "Surely he took up our infirmities and carried our sorrows."

In the Garden of Gethsemane, Jesus prayed, "*Abba*, Father, everything is possible for you. Take this cup from me. Yet not what I will, but what you will" (Mark 14:36). Jesus did not deny his lack of enthusiasm for what lay ahead for him. But he was never angry with God. The Master Teacher is my example for priorities and for how I am to face my own fears.

Prayer partners

Praying for others and receiving their prayers on my behalf was a comfort and a solace.

> *Is any one of you sick? He should call the elders of the church to pray over him and anoint him with oil in the name of the Lord. And the prayer offered in faith will make the sick person well; the Lord will raise him up. If he has sinned, he will be forgiven. Therefore confess your sins to each other and pray for each other so that you may be healed. The prayer of a righteous man is powerful and effective.*
>
> JAMES 5:14–16

When I think about how sad it would be to be relatively alone in a crisis, I'm grateful for the encouragement and prayers of others. Decades later, I'm thankful for the efforts people made to comfort me during my illness. Those friends will always be special to me because they did reach out. They weren't afraid of making a mistake. They had deep, insightful things to say and responded with thoughtful actions. And if they didn't quite get it, they tried. Bless them.

"On him we have set our hope that he will continue to deliver us, as you help us by your prayers. Then many will give thanks on our behalf for the gracious favor granted in answer to the prayers of many" (2 Corinthians 1:10–11). I could literally feel God's strength poured through me because many prayed for me. It is a privilege to carry the names and burdens of others before the throne of the Lord, even as the priests carried the names of the tribes of Israel into the Lord's presence when they entered the Holy of Holies.

> *Some men came carrying a paralytic on a mat and tried to take him into the house to lay him before Jesus. When they could not find a way to do this because of the crowd, they went up on the roof and lowered him on his mat through the tiles into the middle of the crowd, right in front of Jesus.*
>
> LUKE 5:18–19

Sometimes we allow others to carry us to the Savior. In times of crisis we feel too numb to care for ourselves or to pray intelligently. Those who carry us to the Lord are the hands of Jesus to us.

Sometimes we carry others to the Lord in prayer. Praying for others is giving back. It is good therapy.

We are an impatient generation. We want circumstances to change *now*. We want fulfillment in every area of our lives *now*. We don't have time to wait in prayer. We want results instantly.

In contrast, the New Testament is strangely mute about immediate fulfillment and instant spirituality. Instead, we find such words as "perseverance," and "patience." I've been known to pray, asking for patience – *now*. I know a woman who prayed for sixty-eight years for her brother's salvation. When he was eighty years old, he confessed the Lord Jesus as Savior shortly before he died. Imagine the tremendous blessing in that woman's life resulting from decades of faithful praying.

God is working with us and has no intention of dropping us. Prayer is the opportunity for us to partner with God in his perfect plans for us and those we love. His goal is to conform us to the image of his Son. He keeps everlastingly at it because, someday, before all of heaven, he will present us as perfect. That's perseverance. "Now to him who is able to do immeasurably more than all we ask or imagine, according to his power that is at work within us, to him be glory in the church and in Christ Jesus throughout all generations, for ever and ever!" (Ephesians 3:20).

It isn't always easy, however, to see the changes God promises to accomplish in our lives. In watching our children grow, we can't always tell if they have grown from one day to the next. But the marks on our doorpost show that there has been considerable growth over the years.

The Bible speaks of the Christian life as growth which is imperceptible yet constant. Galatians 6:9 says, "Let us not become weary in doing good, for at the proper time we will reap a harvest if we do not give up." Scripture does not say how long we have to wait for our proper time to arrive. What if we must wait a lifetime? So be it. My faithfulness and growth are tied to learning to trust that he will perfect me and you and those we love in his own time.

"Ask and it will be given to you; seek and you will find; knock and the door will be opened to you. For everyone who asks receives; he who seeks finds; and to him who knocks, the door will be opened" (Matthew 7:7–8).

Even in those promises, my view is not God's. He answers my prayers according to his will, according to what he knows is best for me. The answer may be "No." It may be "Wait." It may look very different to what I expected, sometimes so different that I don't recognize it. When I am tempted to fear that God doesn't answer, he assures me that he is a giver of good gifts:

> *Which of you, if his son asks for bread, will give him a stone? Or if he asks for a fish, will give him a snake? If you, then, though you are evil, know how to give good gifts to your children, how much more will your Father in heaven give good gifts to those who ask him!*
>
> MATTHEW 7:9–11

> *Do not be anxious about anything, but in everything, by prayer and petition, with thanksgiving, present requests to God. And the peace of God which transcends all*

*understanding, will guard you hearts and your
minds in Christ Jesus.*

PHILIPPIANS 4:6–7

*Be not forgetful of prayer.
Every time you pray, if your prayer is sincere
there will be new feeling and new meaning in it
which will give you fresh courage
and you will understand that prayer is an education.*

FEDOR DOSTOEVSKY

Pray all the time.

1 THESSALONIANS 5:17, THE MESSAGE

APPLICATION POINT

1. Prayer and worship take many forms. During your prayer time, worship the Lord by singing, clapping your hands, or dancing.

2. The breastplate of the high priests bore twelve precious stones, representing each tribe of Israel. Each time the priest entered the Lord's presence, he brought each tribe before the Lord's remembrance. Like the friends who carried the paralytic to Jesus, who are you carrying to the Lord's remembrance regularly in prayer?

STEPPING OUT

Keep a prayer notebook. Record your requests and note how and when your prayers are answered. This will prove a great comfort when you are struggling and a cause for celebration when you recount God's tangible answers to your requests.

Luis maintains a checkbook where he records prayer requests and notes when they are answered. It is something he has done for fifty years. What a comfort to look back and celebrate the many times God has answered.

Chapter 13

Home Where I Belong

Our help is in the name of the Lord,
the maker of heaven and earth.

Psalm 124:8

I cannot imagine living as though this life is all there is. Life is not fair. This is not heaven. This is a fallen world. We will never really feel comfortable here because it is not our home.

We are eternal beings. We will spend eternity somewhere. God gives us the freedom to choose. People spend eternity either with God or without him – they must choose. It is the most important choice we make in life. Home is a relationship, not merely a destination. Our home is found in a person – Jesus Christ – more than in a place. Jesus is fitting us for heaven and fitting heaven for us. "When everything is ready, I will come and get you, so that you can always be with me where I am" (John 14:1–3, NLT). How amazing that Jesus wants to be with us!

Anxious times bring heaven up close and personal. To me, it was always something I was glad was there, but I didn't know much about it. But there is nothing like cancer to get your attention. And I began to think about heaven because I thought I was going there very, very quickly. I was at the wrong age, it was the wrong kind of cancer, it was too far advanced.

I had almost two years of chemotherapy. And I thought about eternity a lot. I trusted that God would heal me, but if he didn't it was OK by me, because I was going to heaven. I could not believe that diagnosis. I thought it was a mistake. And nobody asked my opinion. But heaven was a reality, and this present life is not. This life is nothing more than basic training for the real thing, which is heaven.

Someone said when we reach heaven we will have two thoughts. The first will be that heaven is so very, very much more amazing than any of us imagined. The second will be, "Why did God have to drag me here kicking and screaming when I could have come running?" It is human nature that we love life and hang on and on and on. We fight God's greatest gift to us.

Could it be that images such as crowns, streets of gold, gems of amazing size and colors, and harps are all mere human efforts to make the inexpressible accessible to our finite minds here and now? As he wrote the book of Revelation, I wonder how often John said, "Well, it was like a..." as he struggled to put into ordinary language the very real future that awaits us in our eternal home.

When we try to imagine heaven, our view is bound to be just a great big, better, amazing, perfect vision of the best we've seen on earth. Though I can't go beyond what is written in God's Word, I choose to trust the One who provided for my access into his presence, to provide me with enough of a vision to make me yearn for that place and that presence. How often we wonder at the infinite detail of God's creation and marvel at what heaven must be like. When I look out at the Pacific Ocean on a clear day, I can't help but say, "How beautiful heaven must be."

My mother has been with Jesus for several years. When she was forty-eight, she contracted polio. One of the last victims after the vaccine was found, she took the sugar cube and a faulty dose gave her the disease she was trying to avoid. She never walked again.

A wheelchair was how my children viewed grandma. They sat on her lap, played around with her chair, and never felt she lacked any grandmothering skills. But she was limited. She could not reach things, get through narrow doorways, or get up stairs. Many times we were told it would be easy to get her into a house or restaurant, when reality proved it was impossible.

But now. Now she walks, runs, lives with no limitations. As much as I miss her, I can't wish her back to things as they were.

Joni Eareckson Tada expressed the same thought:

One day I'm going to leave this wheelchair

behind. I cannot wait. Jesus, You were right
when You said that in this world we would have
trouble because this wheelchair was a lot of
trouble. But the weaker I was in that thing, the
harder I leaned on You. And the harder I leaned
on You, the stronger I discovered You to be.

Modern medications

I'm a shopper. I love to shop. But I've had to learn to control a certain aspect of it. Whenever I'm afraid of a particular activity, I think I will feel better if I just go buy some new clothes. I reason that if I have something new it will give me a boost of self-confidence. This is silly because new clothes are not where my confidence comes from. I've restrained that type of behavior and the Lord has helped me to see it for what it is – profound insecurity.

Everyone feels the same way. We just medicate the feeling differently. Some of us shop. Some eat. Some sleep. Others smoke, drink, or gamble. We escape with television and movies.

Years ago I had to go to a luncheon in Wales where the city council and mayor welcomed Luis and I to the city. I sat beside the elderly mayor, who was wearing his ceremonial chains around his neck. I tried to think of something to talk about, and it didn't go too well. We managed to get through it and at the end he sighed and said, "You know, I was dreading this, and it wasn't that bad at all."

I had been dreading it, too. I had brought new

230

clothes. His comment made me realize all of us are uncomfortable. This is not really our home. We will always feel slightly out of place because things are not really the way they ought to be.

The New Testament uses temporary images of this earthly life. We're described as strangers and pilgrims living in tents. How much more clear could it be? These descriptions are meant to remind us of the temporariness of this transient life:

> *All these people were still living by faith when they died. They did not receive the things promised; they only saw them and welcomed them from a distance. And they admitted that they were aliens and strangers on earth. People who say such things show that they are looking for a country of their own. If they had been thinking of the country they had left, they would have had opportunity to return. Instead, they were longing for a better country – a heavenly one. Therefore God is not ashamed to be called their God, for he has prepared a city for them.*
>
> HEBREWS 11:13–16

Today's believer longs for a thing called community. It is their greatest demand of the church. Go for it! Love it when it is there, but remember, it's fleeting and always a little beyond our reach. That yearning, agony almost, is because this is not heaven. The longer we live, the more we experience life's best and worst, the more our fingers are pried loose from earth's promises, which the hymnist described as, "All the vain things that charm me most."

In regard to ultimate issues of life and eternity, Paul said, "Now we see things imperfectly as in a poor mirror, but then we will see everything with perfect clarity. All that I know now is partial and incomplete, but then I will know everything completely, just as God knows me now" (1 Corinthians 13:12). This principle is true from the most minute issue of the human brain and its function, to the plan of the Trinity in creating man in their image.

New address

Salvation is extravagantly more than a ticket to heaven. More than a get-in-free pass. Our salvation is the beginning of the richest, deepest relationship we will experience. Relationship with God is about having life and having it abundantly now and for eternity:

> *And this is eternal life: (it means) to know (to perceive, recognize, become acquainted with and understand) You, the only true and real God, and (likewise) to know Him, Jesus (as the) Christ, the Anointed One, the Messiah, Whom You have sent.*
> JOHN 17:3, AMPLIFIED BIBLE

It is a reciprocal relationship:

> *(For my determined purpose is) that I may know Him – that I may progressively become more*

deeply and intimately acquainted with Him,
perceiving and recognizing and understanding
(the wonders of His Person) more strongly and
more clearly. And that I may in that same way
come to know the power outflowing from His
resurrection (which it exerts over believers);
and that I may so share His sufferings as to
be continually transformed (in spirit into His
likeness even) to His death.

PHILIPPIANS 3:10, AMPLIFIED BIBLE

Heaven is the culmination of today's commitment to the place and authority of God and his Word in our life.

The Bible does not give a picture of a smooth, easy ride straight to heaven. Sometimes I ask, "Oh, Lord Jesus, how long?" There is a parenthesis between our birth and our arrival in heaven – it's called life. And life gets messy. That's where our struggles and difficult experiences come in. Life is a boot camp for eternity. I am learning through pressures, pain, and worrisome possibilities and realities to trust God and remember that the world will never satisfy you or me. Our identity is that of a citizen of heaven here on assignment as a loving ambassador for the King of kings.

It is not morbid to plan ahead for the day of adversity by developing a strong faith and trust in the Lord Jesus Christ. We enjoy life here once we settle eternity. Subscribe today to God's insurance policy – see Psalm 91. C. S. Lewis said no one is prepared to live life here until he is prepared to live life in heaven.

Years ago when I had cancer, a friend assembled a collection of scriptures, hymns, and poems that gave me courage when I was scared to death. It is a gift that I still refer to.

Jesus didn't say, "Be brave." He said, "Trust me – I have a master plan." Trust is a practice in which we learn to leave our fears at his feet through prayer. He doesn't say, "Try not to be troubled." He says, "Don't do it. Don't be troubled." It means that it is possible to control fear. We are not asked to do what we cannot do. How unfair that would be!

"You trust in God; trust also in me" (John 14:1). The disciples were afraid he would leave. They did not want a quick hug, bye-bye, and "I'm gone, do your best and try to remember what I taught you." Jesus wanted them to be grounded in reality. "You trust the Father; now trust me." When we have studied the attributes of God, we are prepared when bad things happen. He says there are many rooms in his house. One thing we learn in walking through this life is that homelessness is not an issue of having a roof over our head. Lots of people feel homeless when they have a home, an apartment, a house, a flat, or someplace where they live. But they have a sense of not being grounded, of being rootless.

We have an eternal home in the heavens. Where we belong (heaven) reveals who we are, not what we do. Many people belong to associations, and clubs, even to a church, which is an earthly picture of heaven, but they still do not feel like they have a home. The home where we really belong is where the Father is.

Heavenly relationship

A friend of mine says she doesn't care where she travels or lives, as long as her family is with her. It is the relationship that is home for her.

"There are two things we cannot do alone," said Paul Tournier. "One is to be married, the other is to be a Christian." From time to time young families will loosely attach themselves to our extended family, especially for holidays. The reason is usually that they are living here in our community, attending our church, but are a continent away from their own family. This leads to a great yearning for what we call community, or even putting down roots. This is a uniquely modern phenomenon. We are far more transient and mobile than our grandparents.

Heaven is where we really belong. Still, we should be sensitive to that hollow yearning in all of us, to belong. There are days when we feel we don't fit, and look inward. I choose to look upward and remember that the meaning and purpose of my life, in many ways, is that I might make the transition from earth to heaven smoothly.

A newspaper headline reported, "Homeless lack more than shelter – they want a place of their own." Today's rootless Christian longs for community. It is worth the effort to create community, and to appreciate it when we find it, but we should also remember that it's always slightly beyond our grasp because heaven is our one true home.

"We are confident, I say, and would prefer to be

away from the body and at home with the Lord. So we make it our goal to please him, whether we are at home in the body or away from it" (2 Corinthians 5:8–9). All of this talk about preferring to be with God in heaven may seem a bit emotional, but Paul says, "And by the way, as long as I'm here, I make it my aim to please him." Home is found in a person more than a place. Home is found in the person of Jesus Christ.

So what does this all mean? What am I here for? I'm here to better know God so that the transition from here to heaven is not such a big leap. I'll feel like I'm not meeting a stranger. The character-building activities are to make me more like Jesus. Romans 8:28–29 says that things work together not necessarily happily, but so that I might be conformed into the image of God's Son, so that heaven will seem natural.

Following Christ, being a Christian, is a relationship. It is you and me belonging to God's family. We are joint heirs with Jesus and heaven is our home. "That you also may be where I am," Jesus said (John 14:3). Whether I die, or Jesus comes for me at his second coming, his statement is true. I'll not walk that path without the One who promised to be with me in the journey.

"I will come again." It's a promise. Did you notice what he said? There are many sweet invitations from Jesus: "Come to me, all you who are weary and burdened, and I will give you rest" (Matthew 11:28). There's an old spiritual song that says, "Everybody talkin' about Heaven ain't goin' there." And in the kind of world we live in, it is not politically correct to make statements like that. But heaven is the place for the children of God in the same way that my house is for the children of Palau.

In the evenings, I would stand on the front porch and call to my children to come in for supper. My children came. No others. In the same way, Jesus issues to us invitation after invitation. But home is for the members of the family. "To all those who received him, to those who believed in his name, he gave the right to become children of God" (John 1:12). You can admire the gospel, the Good News, and say how wonderful it is, but at some point, you need to respond.

We don't earn the right to heaven. Heaven is a gift of God's grace, gained for us because Christ Jesus took away our sins on the cross. We are God's children by relationship, not by deeds and action. I have children and grandchildren, and I love them all. But they are related by blood. And that's the way God set it up. Jesus shed his blood, and we are related to him by blood relationship. "If you confess with your mouth, 'Jesus is Lord,' and believe in your heart that God raised him from the dead, you will be saved" (Romans 10:9). We are at that moment adopted into God's family. We become joint heirs with God's Son.

Part of the family

A Christian is a child of God by the new birth, by adoption into his family. And there are certain rights and privileges to being a part of God's family. The greatest help we can extend to others is to invite them to heaven, to introduce them to Jesus Christ, to mentor them in their relationship with God.

A music teacher introduces the student to an instrument. Weekly, the instructor meets with the student and teaches technique for playing the instrument and for reading the printed music. Together, the teacher and student explore genres, timing, and dynamics. At the end of each year, the student plays a well-rehearsed piece for an audience of peers, fans, and loved ones. From year to year, the recital showcases the new level the student has achieved. Bible study, Sunday school, and church are weekly teaching times where the student of God learns more about our relationship with the heavenly Father. Each year we can mark spiritual growth in our own lives as well as in the lives of those we mentor on a regular basis through prayer and study of the Scriptures. Ironically, the more we are settled about heaven as our permanent home, the more successful our life here on earth becomes.

Jesus is our example. He conquered death and is preparing a home for you and me in heaven. Most religious leaders have tombs, monuments to what they were. The Lord Jesus had no tomb and we are his monuments.

In this temporary, fallen world, housed in these temporary, fallen bodies, we experience suffering. The discomfort of suffering comes from four sources:

• Ourselves as a consequence of our sin, mistakes, and accidents.

• The attacks of Satan, the enemy of our souls and bodies.

• The world's fallen side, consisting of illnesses and imperfections.

• God's use of trials to strengthen, teach, mature, and toughen us.

The more closely I seek to follow the Lord Jesus, the more I hear his voice and respond appropriately. When I do not appreciate a pressure situation, I pray, "Lord, let me learn what you have for me in this – quickly!" And I'd like to not learn this again.

In John 14:2, Jesus said, "I am going there to prepare a place for you." Someday he'll come back and take us to heaven. The local assembly of believers, the church, is a training-ground for the heaven that will be ours one day. Until Christ returns, the church is where God has put each of us to bless and be blessed. Exercise your gifts. Find your place. It's important.

As I put fear in its place, which is in the capable hands of Jesus, I move into a mature relationship with my God. Looking forward to finishing this life's race well, I've made a list of what I'm not going to do:

• Totally ignore fashion trends.

• Refuse to admit I can't hear perfectly or remember so well.

• Compare prescription minutiae. I don't remember the names of the medicines I take – just that there are four.

• Continue to recite local history to people who haven't the maturity to catch its importance or aren't that interested.

Here's a list of characteristics of those who finish well:

• They have perspective which enables them to focus.

• They enjoy intimacy with Christ and experience repeated times of inner renewal.

• They are disciplined in important areas of life.

• They continue to learn new things.

• They have a network of meaningful relationships including younger adults and children.

• They continue to mentor and be mentored.

• They are not convinced that they are always right.

Therefore we do not lose heart. Though outwardly we are wasting away, yet inwardly we are being renewed day by day. For our light and momentary troubles are achieving for us an eternal glory that far outweighs them all. So we fix our eyes not on what is seen, but on what is unseen. For what is seen is temporary, but what is unseen is eternal.

2 CORINTHIANS 4:16–18

The years we are gifted with are years to know Jesus better. How sad to be old, and have gained nothing useful from life to pass on or use myself. Ephesians 5:15–17 (J. B. Phillips) says:

> *Live life, then, with a new sense of*
> *responsibility, not as men who do not know the*
> *meaning and purpose of life, but as those who*
> *do. Make the best use of your time, despite all*
> *the difficulty of these days. Don't be vague but*
> *firmly grasp what you know to be the will of the*
> *Lord.*

The way home

How do we find our way home? God showed the Israelites the way through the desert by leading them with a pillar of fire by night and a cloud by day. Trusting and obeying, the travelers found their fear dissolved as their anticipation grew. Ready to cross the Jordan into the Promised Land, the priests led the way, carrying the Ark of the Covenant, which was the symbol of God's presence. "When you see the ark of the covenant of the Lord your God, and the priests, who are Levites, carrying it, you are to move out from your positions and follow it. Then you will know which way to go, since you have never been this way" (Joshua 3:3–4).

This passage of Old Testament Scripture reminds me that the symbolism that I have cherished, and sung in our hymns, isn't quite accurate. I'm sure a lot of good minds have realized this before. We think of the Jordan River – over which the children of Israel crossed to enter the Promised Land, Canaan – as symbolic of death. That is, a crossing, in the plan of God, into the place of blessing. That symbol could work, except that it demands that Canaan would have to be heaven.

Canaan was no heaven. On the contrary, it was a place of battle and conflict. It was potentially full of good things, but it had to be conquered. It was theirs, but not without struggle. All the enemies had to be rooted out. In my thinking, it is more a picture of the Christian life. We cross that Jordan, into the family of God, but then we encounter the conflicts and enemies that need to be conquered.

Fear is one of those enemies, and it is conquered in the name of the Lord God. It is not a one-time battle but a series of skirmishes ending in total victory when we cross the river of death into a life without any cause for fear, with the Lord Jesus in heaven.

We experience the same as we follow the Word of God. The Bible is the Lord's communication to us today. It outlines the way we are to follow on our journey to our Promised Land, heaven.

With the presence of the Holy Spirit with me and dwelling within me, I can face what comes. There is a still, small voice which says, "And surely I am with you always, to the very end of the age" (Matthew 28:20). If he is with me, right up until my final breath on this earth, what is it I am afraid of? The step beyond the end of the world, for me, is his presence. Tough times remind me that this world is not all that great. It is tinged with sadness, its best is always up for comparison with the past, or the dreamy future which may never come. The Bible calls life a vale of tears. We were made for heaven, and nothing else will satisfy.

Time is a limited resource. May we spend it with eternity's values in view. Family matters, and there is nothing like our presence to encourage with word and deed, to encourage others to put the bondage of fear aside and live full out. Studies show that when Christian residents of retirement facilities are interviewed, they consistently say two things. First, looking back over their lives, they wish they had lived less fearfully. Secondly, they wish they had done more to expand the kingdom of God. Life is to be spent, not saved. We choose how we will invest our days. Fear is a cruel master and not worthy of our allegiance.

Even in those challenging situations when my first reaction is to be fearful, I've learned there are five things I can bank on:

- Life is tough.

- God knows everything.

- God cares.

- God is good.

- Heaven is sure.

The greatest help we can give to people is to invite them to heaven. There is true stability. To ask Christ to be your Lord and Savior, or to renew your relationship with him, you can pray something like this:

Lord Jesus, thank you for what you have said about heaven. Thank you for dying on the cross for my sins. Forgive me. Thank you for the access I have to a deep relationship with you now, and a home in heaven. Thank you for promising to be always with me. Deliver me from fear, worry, dread of a future that you have in your loving care. Help me today to be confident of my place in the family of God and my destiny.

I sought the Lord, and he answered me;
he delivered me from all my fears.
Those who look to him are radiant;
their faces are never covered with shame.

PSALM 34:4–5

APPLICATION POINT

In eternity, I will not be asked about my awards, my bank account, the square footage of my house, or the degrees after my name. Only two questions are likely to come up. Can you answer these questions honestly?

- What did you do with the gifts God gave to you?

- Did you bring anyone with you?

Highlight comforting Scripture verses in your Bible. Then you'll be able to find them quickly when you need them. You'll also know where to direct someone else who is scared to death.

Stepping out

Read books by the great Christian thinkers Philip Yancey, Amy Carmichael, and C. S. Lewis. Encourage a child with the book, *Am I Trusting?* by Jeanie St John Taylor.

CHAPTER 14

WHEN ALL IS SAID AND DONE

I waited patiently for the Lord;
he turned to me and heard my cry.
He lifted me out of the slimy pit,
out of the mud and mire;
he set my feet on a rock
and gave me a firm place to stand.
He put a new song in my mouth,
a hymn of praise to our God.
Many will see and fear
and put their trust in the Lord.
Blessed is the man
who makes the Lord his trust,
who does not look to the proud,
to those who turn aside to false gods.
Many, O Lord my God,
are the wonders you have done.
The things you planned for us
no one can recount to you;

were I to speak and tell of them,
they would be too many to declare.

PSALM 40:1–5

What encouragement do we find from the Lord? What is the Good News? The great news is that there is a progression going on here, a development that frees us from fear and its outworking torment. We are daily being freed from fear and into perfect love. We are not there yet.

To become perfect in love will be wonderful, but lest we become impatient or frustrated, we need to remember that we're in a process. It is a question of stages. That's why I love the Scripture's use of human birth and growth patterns as illustrations. We are not born full grown. Though Adam and Eve were formed full grown, the rest of us are born as small, helpless infants. As we grow, we are encouraged to walk, placing one wobbling foot in front of another. It is a basic concept that we all understand – all cultures in all generations. As parents, we remind ourselves that so many stages of childhood are merely passing, simply outgrown.

As a follower of Jesus Christ begins this process of being perfected in love, the fear and negativity that we practiced in the past is submitted to God's love and his plan for us. Even the idea of maturity gives room for childhood, adolescence, and adulthood. As adults, we continue to mature (1 John 1:12–14). No one criticizes a baby for his baby ways. But growth is expected. A forty-year-old baby is sad and pathetic.

A believer's growth and maturity in the faith has much to do with his ability to deal with fear in healthy ways. When we were outside the family of God, we lived saturated by fear, knowing nothing of God's love. When we came to trust Christ, we found a perplexing mixture of fear and faith in our hearts. But as we grow in fellowship with the Father, gradually the fear recedes, no longer coloring our mind and emotions. Decision-making becomes dominated by the One within us, who is perfect love.

An immature Christian is tossed back and forth between fear and confident love; a mature Christian rests in God's love:

> *If any of you lacks wisdom, he should ask God, who gives generously to all without finding fault, and it will be given to him. But when he asks, he must believe and not doubt, because he who doubts is like a wave of the sea, blown and tossed by the wind. That man should not think he will receive anything from the Lord; he is a double-minded man, unstable in all he does.*

JAMES 1:5–8

As our faith strengthens, with John we say, "perfect love casts out fear." I like the idea that fear doesn't just shift a little, maybe over to the side. It is driven out. Completely cast out.

In most respects I am grateful for the time and place where God placed me, but occasionally I think about what it might have been like to be a wife and mother, oh, say a hundred years ago. Hard work comes to mind immediately. Tedious hard work.

But there is a good side to boring, repetitive activities. A hidden value. They give you and me time to think. The problem with today is that we have figured out how to multi-task and if it's boring, I ain't doing it. I have things to do, and places to go. But, when and where can I think? Where can I work on my fears? When can I meditate on a message I heard in church that resonated in my soul? I can't contemplate deeply if I never have five empty minutes to think. Then the frenzied cycle of fear and reaction continues, and I live my life scared to death.

I am not averse to a little boring housework. I've found value in simple, repetitive tasks where my hands automatically move through the familiar, freeing my mind to ponder. That's where I figure things out, sort the real issues versus the nagging, unworthy ideas that just won't go away. I do my best thinking when:

   • Driving (part of my brain should be geared to the task).

   • Walking (not as exercise, necessarily – just getting from one place to another).

   • Gardening.

   • Ironing (my personal hands-on favorite, though I know this is not popular with younger generations). This is a good venue for working out fearful thoughts and scenarios, because

I often come out of my wonderful laundry room and say to my husband, "I know what we should do." The peace comes because, in doing something that has to be done but does not require concentration, I am free to talk things over with Jesus.

Center on Christ

Modern life tends to leave us with scattered, incomplete segments of assessment. I remember something, start to think in the Lord's presence, review the issue, and get interrupted. Much later, I start it up all over again. Men and women in previous times had a precious privilege of long, uninterrupted meditation to work through the fears that plague us all. David, the shepherd boy, in those sustained, boring periods alone with sheep, has given us the kind of thoughts birthed when there is nothing between ourselves and the Savior. David's reflections and insights are recorded in the Psalms. Because he had the time, he wrote and we are blessed.

In the same way God taught David about himself then, our precious Lord cherishes relationship with us today. Some good friends of ours experienced a primal fear – what if my baby is not born whole and healthy? The mother said:

We were given a diagnosis of a very rare genetic syndrome. We were devastated, broken-hearted, grieved. There is debate about the actual name of our daughter's situation, but it doesn't matter to us because the treatment of the seizures does not change, nor does our incredible love for her. She has truly changed our lives. Although so powerless at only six months old, she has powerfully changed our hearts and taught us to know her Creator:

• God does not make mistakes.

• God wants us to trust him and surrender our lives to him.

• God holds onto us as we hold onto him.

• Strength is perfected in weakness.

• God is trustworthy.

• We are so grateful for all his gifts – especially each other.

• Our suffering will be used for good.

• God does not leave us or forsake us.

• God collects our tears and cares about each one of them.

God's purpose is that our fears would make us not bitter, but better.

In modern life we often hear the term, "exit strategy." It has to do with planning events, wars, a business, or life in general, including an initial plan, the execution of the plan, and then getting out cleanly and wisely. An older person passing on the family business needs to have spent much time thinking of the exit strategy. Most aspects of life have a conclusion, and it can be magnificent. Or messy.

As I worked on this book about fear, I thought about how life works. Many additional themes emerged as I reminisced through my adventure with fears, both silly and serious. As a teenager I memorized these verses from the Psalms: "This poor girl cried, and the Lord heard her, and delivered her from all her fears" (Psalm 34:4, 6, my own wording). Indeed, he did. Bit by bit. Slowly.

Looking back, I do not want to end with any serious question marks. Recently Luis and I viewed a DVD of our friend, Cliff Barrows, looking back over his life and ministry with the Billy Graham Team. We were touched, and Luis turned to me and said, "Now, do you have that in your book – the faithfulness of God?"

I hope so. I want to conclude this book in a way that encourages those who have miles to go. The hymn, "Great is Thy Faithfulness," was sung at our wedding, along with "Savior, Like a Shepherd Lead Us." God is faithful. He has led us.

My early youthful fears had to do with:

• I would never marry – at least not well.

• I wouldn't have children.

• I wouldn't have blessed children.

• I might not bless the world and accomplish my goals.

• I might not survive life-threatening illnesses and dangers.

All I can say, along with the hymnist, is, "All the way my Savior leads me, what have I to ask beside?"

I'm thankful for the godly people we've known, the works of God we've seen, the people we've nudged into God's family, and the overwhelming presence of the Holy Spirit when the unthinkable feared thing happens. Great is his faithfulness.

This little girl learned, "I will trust, and not be afraid."

Join me, won't you?

"Because he loves me," says the Lord, "I will rescue him;
I will protect him, for he acknowledges my name.
He will call upon me, and I will answer him;
I will be with him I trouble,
I will deliver him and honor him.
With long life will I satisfy him
and show him my salvation.

PSALM 91:14–16

APPLICATION POINT

1. Where have you seen God's hand of comfort and protection in your life?

2. What can you praise God for today?

STEPPING OUT

Highlight God's comforting promises in a Bible. Give the Bible to someone who is struggling with fear.

The Luis Palau Association

Since their marriage in 1961, Pat Palau and her husband, evangelist Luis Palau, have dedicated their lives to the worldwide proclamation of the Good News of Jesus Christ. Having lived in four countries on two continents, they have reached more than 1 billion people through evangelistic events and media campaigns.

Now known as the Luis Palau Association, this worldwide ministry exists to proclaim the Good News of Jesus Christ, to teach the Church the principles of victorious Christian living through the power of the Holy Spirit, and equip the next generation to hold high the banner of biblical Christianity.

Palau Festivals – what the ministry is most well-known for – have produced some of the largest audiences ever recorded in cities from South Florida to South America; from Europe to Asia. In addition, the ministry includes daily radio programs, television specials, the Next Generation Alliance (created to grow and nurture partner evangelists) and Livin It (an initiative begun by one of their sons to reach today's youth through action sports).

For more information about the Luis Palau Association and how you can be involved in its worldwide ministry, visit www.palau.org.

Also, to gain access to articles, audio messages, videos, and more than 40 years worth of valuable evangelistic resources, visit the Change Your World online community at http://change.palau.org.